I0410500

TIMELESS

WRITINGS

#29

A COMPILATION
FOR MANY WRITERS

TATAY JOBO ELIZES
COMPILER, NOV. 2016

Published: Nov. 2016

Self-Publisher/Compiler/Printer

Tatay Jobo Elizes, born 1934 in Manila, now senior ctizen in Brooklyn, NY. Besides self-publishing, he is busy in piglets dispersal programs for livelihood projects in the Philippines.
.

Acknowledgement

Gratitude and acknowledgment belongs to all contributing writers who gave their permission to compile all articles in a book like this to record history based on timely events that directly or indirectly affect our lives. Copyrights of each article belong to the particular author and he/she is free to re-publish anywhere, without any restriction.

Dedication

I dedicate this book to **all Filipinos** all over the world and to my immediate family, friends and relatives.

This book has the following ISBN numbers:
ISBN-13: 978 - 1539825586
& ISBN-10: 1539825582

Disclaimer:

Views are expressed by the authors alone. Tatay Jobo Elizes does not knowingly publish false information or commit copyright infringement having been given explicit permission to publish these writings. Tatay Jobo Elizes may not be held liable for the views of the authors exercising his/her right to free expression.

Free pdf file

FREE reading as ebook is available to interested parties. Just email me at **job_elizes@yahoo.com.**

Booklist Websites

http.//tinyurl.com/mj76ccq
www.jobelizes6.wix.com/mysit

Contents

--ooo--

1.

The Philippines Under Duterte: A Communist Nightmare?

Gene Alcantara

(Immigration Adviser/Caseworker at Alcantara Consultancy Services. Finished M.A. degree at Oxford Brookes U. Lives in London. Lived in Warsaw, Poland. Origin, San Pablo City)

Timeline, Oct. 11, 2016, His facebook

There is a nightmare hovering over the Philippines and it gives me heart palpitations -- the prospect of being converted into a communist country by the new administration of President Rodrigo Duterte.

The prospects are very real, and the country appears to be being prepared to be skinned and boiled alive, ready to be served on a bamboo platter to our would be China communist masters.

Why else would President Duterte keep coming up with all these inane comments, taunting and swearing at the Philippines' traditional allies such as the USA and the European Union? Even the United Nations. Why does he keep repeating he wants to cut ties with them?

Is it not because he is trying to obfuscate what he seems to be really trying to do, which is to get the country under the influence, if not the actual control, of Communist China? This is my nightmare scenario.

The signs are already abundant, even before Duterte' s election and in his first 100 days --

1. He has been praising China (and Russia, a former communist country) throughout his 100 days.

2. He has practically given up our West Philippine Sea territories to China, despite the Hague ruling and the hard work put in by the Aquino administration in defending the islands.

3. He keeps kowtowing to China.

4. He has been promising them good deals in exchange for highways and infrastructure in Mindanao.

5. He wants to join the China-founded development bank for Asia.

6. He admitted paying tax to the New People's Army and he seems friendly with the communist rebels, even appearing in pictorials. They have also released hostages to him.

7. He has been pushing for peace with the National Democratic Front/NPA which I understand are heavily influenced by Chinese communism.

His constant attacks on the Catholic Church, the Bishops, even the Pope, seem to be scripted and aimed at preparing the country for a godless republic, which communist countries have been or are. Especially glaring is his comparison of himself to God, which people appear not to have reacted to.

Only his comparison of Hitler's massacre of Jews to his own desire to slaughter 3 million Filipinos drew widespread condemnation, especially overseas. He has since apologized for this but Teddy Locsin, his Ambassador to the UN, has been continuing the theme.

These no longer sound like a madman raving, but are clever diversions to distract us from the real issues and so that we do not notice what he is actually doing, which is selling out to China.

Even his war on drugs and the mass extra judicial/vigilante killings now appear part of a wider plan. Everyone is too appalled to care about anything else. We have become so benumbed by his words and actions that we might end up not caring anymore, or that we might be too beaten to submission to protest or fight anymore.

The general public are already oppressed by the situation. Political dissent is effectively suppressed as even the majority in the Senate are cowed into silence, and the Lower House of Congress barely squeaks. Only Senators Leila de Lima and Antonio Trillanes IV show some real backbone and are thereby constantly being attacked and vilified by Duterte' s cohorts.

Duterte has repeated his threat to declare Martial Law, following his recent State of lawlessness. But I did not see any public protestations. If he pushes through with this, will he be able to turn the country more easily into a communist state, with equality among the general public, but under the control of an elite Duterte Politburo, backed by a Ministry of State Security or some similar Chekha/KGB style secret police? It is horrible to contemplate a 90 year old Dictator

Duterte propped up by Martial Law, continuing with his bloody war on Filipino druggies.

The military meanwhile is very, very quiet.

The press meanwhile is under attack and journalists and their families are threatened by online trolls, in an attempt to muzzle them.

Even Overseas Filipinos who post or share anything critical about Duterte on social media very quickly get inundated by negative comments by online trolls who call them yellow or paid or some other nasty name. Some of these are known die-hard Duterte supporters, although the attacks are less vicious now in Europe as they probably realize they could be reported to overseas police authorities for threatening behaviour or harassment.

The question really is why is Duterte doing all these? Is it ideology because he is really a closet Communist? Is he trying to hoodwink everyone by getting them too busy with worrying about his dirty mouth, that everyone misses his real goal -- which is to turn our country Communist? Remember that he was a student of Jose Ma Sison, NDF head and long term exile in Utrecht, Netherlands and the two appear to be really good friends if not comrades.

But if he is a closet communist, why then is he fanatically loyal to the Marcos family? He may have received huge financial assistance from them in his quest for national power, so paying them back is understandable (ie burying the elder Marcos in the Heroes' Cemetery, and naming the younger Marcos as his successor) but it is still an enigma because he is doing this against the wishes of Marcos' Martial Law victims and their families.

He probably received similar assistance from China, and using the logic of paying them back as he is doing with the Marcoses might explain his blind support for them. But clearly it would have been probably a much larger amount that he is now willing to sell our sovereignty for peanuts.

As President, Duterte could be doing so much good for the country if only he would focus on the needs of the country. Yes, clean up the drugs problem, but not at the expense of hapless human lives.

Tackle poverty, improve the economy, assist Overseas Filipinos in need. He may not be the best, but he could be an adequate leader.

Instead he appears hell-bent on turning the country upside down, on cleansing its population, and realigning it with China in particular.

The test for him is probably the next natural disaster that is bound to hit the Philippines, it being one of the most disaster prone countries of the world. During Typhoon Haiyan/Yolanda, the top donor overseas governments who provided aid are listed below [Source: PCIJ article, GMA News Online, 15/01/2015]. The list should provide pause for thought to President Duterte and his officials.

1. United Kingdom US$121 million
2. United States US$ 90 million
3. Australia US$ 64 million
4. Japan US$ 64 million
5. Canada US$ 59 million
6. Germany US$ 40 million
7. Norway US$ 32 million
8. United Arab Emirates US$ 21 million
9. China US$ 16 million
10. Sweden US$ 15 million
11. Russia [no figure readily available]
12. United Nations Agencies US$ 81 million

13. European Community US$ 49 million

Whatever Duterte' s endgame might be, I have no doubt it will continue to be bloody and end life as we know it as a democratic society, if he does not change his ways.

This is the time when we freedom-loving Filipinos, whether back home or overseas, need to be ever vigilant. When we see the signs, we need to raise our voices to get heard in protest against being hoodwinked into becoming a bailiwick of China. Or even becoming like communist China.

President Duterte has also been making positive noises towards a surprised Russia. Once they get over the fact that the Philippine President appears to be veering away from the American sphere of influence, we might see Russia getting bolder in its engagement with the country. Russia's focus had been Europe, but it could very well get involved in Southeast Asia. It was known to have been involved before as the former communist Union of Soviet Socialist Republics in Vietnam against the Americans.

Actually we all just need to wake ourselves up from this communist nightmare and realize that something bad is already happening to our beloved country, and that it will get worse if we, the wider populace both in and out of the country, just kept quiet and buried our heads in the proverbial sands.

Duterte has been talking about crossing the Rubicon to the "other side of the ideological barrier."

We must do all we can to stop it.

-ooo-

2.

Ad Lib:
DUTERTE-ISMS

Greg B. Macabenta

*Greg B. Macabenta is an advertising
and communications man shuttling between San
Francisco and Manila and providing unique insights
on issues from both perspectives.
gregmacabenta@hotmail.com*

Timeline, Oct 24, 2016
Moonglowplanet site

Anyone with a relatively good grasp of current events can tell you who said this: "Ask not what your country can do for you but what you can do for your country." Or this: "We have nothing to fear but fear itself." The first one was John F. Kennedy's classic statement on his inauguration as president of the United States. The second was by President Franklin Delano Roosevelt in his inaugural address at the height of the Great Depression in America. What about this? "My loyalty to my party ends where my loyalty to my country begins." That was President Manuel Luis

Quezon, making the patriotic statement that Philippine new politicians have since slightly adjusted to: "My loyalty to my party ends where my loyalty to the newly installed president begins."

We usually remember prominent personalities by the classic quips they make. President Ramon Magsaysay will always be remembered for declaring, "Those who have less in life should have more in law." And Senate President Jose Avelino of Samar's candid quip will forever be part of Philippine political lore: "What are we in power for?" President Joseph "Erap" Estrada's solemn inaugural vow -- "Walang kama-kamag -anak, walang kai-kaibigan" -- will always stand out as the epitome of political untruthfulness, compared to the stark naked truthfulness of Senator Miriam Defensor-Santiago's admission, "I lied!" This was her response when asked why she did not make good her threat to jump off a plane over the Luneta, in connection with her stout defense of Erap. But all of these quotable quotes now pale compared to this one: "Putang inang Santo Papa." That, of course, is vintage Rodrigo Roa Duterte, President of the Republic of the Philippines. Hopefully -- and I am sincerely one of those with this hope -- Duterte will be remembered in Philippine history as the President who instituted genuine positive change in the country, curbed criminality, particularly the drug menace, minimized corruption in government, untangled the infernal Metro Manila traffic, built adequate infrastructure to meet the needs not only of businesses and urban folk but also those in the rural areas, and finally enabled the poor to share in the benefits of economic prosperity. Unfortunately, whatever good Duterte might notch will likely trigger a corresponding snicker over his classic foot-in-mouth gaffes. And that is the sad part. I am tempted to paraphrase Mark Antony's eulogy for Julius Caesar: "The mistakes that Presidents commit live after them. The achievements are oft interred with their bones." Frankly, I am beginning to believe that Duterte sincerely wants to leave a proud legacy as President of our country. And considering that a six-year term is really not enough to institute lasting changes, I can also understand his tendency to take short cuts, including extrajudicial ones. As an account management person in an ad agency servicing an unforgiving client, I was known to tell my assistants: "If you face a blank wall, go around it, go over it or go under it. If none of that works, break down the goddamn wall." Apparently Duterte has the same attitude. Unfortunately, if you were to go by his public statements -- which he, at one time, characterized as preposterous -- you would feel like the passenger of a sports car negotiating a zigzag mountain road at top speed. You have the hairy feeling that the vehicle could jump off the cliff at the next turn. The latest Duterte-ism is his threat to withdraw the Philippines from membership in the United Nations, over his pique at the UN's disapproval of his murderous methods in his war against the drug menace. Wrote CNN: "Filipino President Rodrigo Duterte insulted and threatened to leave the United Nations in response to criticism of his approach to drug crime since taking office...'Maybe we'll just have to decide to separate from the United Nations,' he said in English during the address. 'If you are that insulting, son of a bitch, we should just leave,' he said then in Tagalog, according to a translation by CNN Philippines. 'Take us out of your organization. You have done nothing anyway.'" Duterte appears to have conveniently forgotten the humanitarian aid for the Philippines organized by the United Nations and its agencies in the wake of super-typhoon Yolanda and how our country depends on international support in our dispute with China over the Spratlys. But this is vintage foot-in-mouth, shoot-from-the-lip Duterte. His allies in Congress have been stumbling all over themselves to rush to his defense, pointing out that he should not be taken seriously.

Here's how the dailies reported on it: "At least two senators think so, saying President Duterte's threat to withdraw the Philippines from the United Nations should not be taken too seriously. "I don't take it seriously. We are one of [the United Nations'] founding members,' Senate Minority Leader Ralph Recto said on Sunday... "Sen. Sherwin Gatchalian said he believed Mr. Duterte knew that leaving the United Nations would be detrimental to the Philippines.

"'He is a very intelligent man. Leaving the UN will throw our nation back to the Stone Age. He knows very well that being an isolationist country is not in the best interest of the Filipino people,' he said on Sunday." Did Recto and Gatchalian realize that they were, in effect, being patronizing towards the President of the country and insulting his intelligence?

But this is not the first time that Duterte's people have, in effect, dismissed their bosses' statements as virtual hot air. About Duterte's vow to curb criminality and solve the problem of illegal drugs in three to six months, Philippine National Police Chief Ronald de la Rosa clarified: "Hindi namin makuha yan talaga yan 100%. Siguro kung mabagsak man kami maabot kami ng 60% lang o 70%. (We cannot achieve 100%. Maybe we can reach 60% or 70%.)" My own reaction to Duterte's overreaching claim was to say that the country should be happy enough if he actually succeeded in reducing criminality, particularly illegal drug trafficking.

In fact, Duterte himself has been self-deprecating and has cautioned the media against taking all his public statements "seriously."

When human rights activists accused him, during the presidential campaign, of being behind the killings of 700 suspected criminals in Davao, Duterte corrected that and claimed, "1,700."

He subsequently told the media in Davao City, shortly before assuming the presidency: "If it is a preposterous, ridiculous or out of the blue statement, kalabitin mo yung taga-Davao. Sabihin mo lang, 'anong sinasabi ng loko-lokong ito?' (Ask the folks in Davao, what is this crazy fellow saying?)" When asked how would people know if he was serious or just joking, Duterte replied,"If it's ridiculous, ano ba 'tong gago? (Am I stupid?)" Anyone interested in trivia could compile the fast-enlarging list of Duterte-isms and write a book. And to that book, if it is ever published, I would like to contribute a fictitious situation where Duterte points a gun at a suspect and warns, "Patyon ta ka! (I will kill you.)" After Duterte pulls the trigger and the victim collapses, the dying man mutters: "Akala ko hindi serious! (I thought he was not serious.)"

-ooo-

3.

Digong was the 'Manchurian Candidate' all along!

Perry Diaz

Perry Diaz started publishing Balita *as a community newsletter in 1987. Over the years, his commentaries and viewpoints have become increasingly popular with Pinoys in the United States, Philippines and abroad. In 2003, Perry started publishing his opinion articles by the name of* Perryscope. *Today,* Global Balita *is a daily-published online culmination of* Perryscopes, *social commentaries, news and features from a variety of respected sources about Filipinos and all that affect them.*

Dateline, Oct. 24, 2016, PerryScope - Featured, Opinion

In **Philippine** elections, presidential candidates are labeled according to their perceived political persuasion or ideological beliefs. However, political persuasion doesn't really matter in

Philippine politics because Filipino politicians change their political affiliations to suit their personal objectives. There are the "Amboys" (American Boys). There are the "balimbings" (political turncoats and opportunists). And there are the "Manchurian Candidates" (secretly aligned with China).

Then Mayor Rodrigo Duterte meets with Chinese Consul General Song Ronghua (left) and his party during their courtesy call at Marco Polo Hotel during the presidential campaign. (Credit: Bing Gonzales)

The Philippines, which is considered pro-American in every meaning of the word, has always been allied with the U.S., politically, economically, militarily, and culturally (there are five million Filipinos living in the U.S.) since she gained independence from Mother America in 1946. But "independence" from America hasn't really been deeply rooted because of the interdependence of the two countries on matters of foreign policy, economics, and national defense, so much so that the Philippine government didn't see the need for a strong navy and air force to defend her sovereignty and territorial integrity.

With three defense agreements that exist between the two countries – Mutual Defense Treaty (MDT), Visiting Forces Agreement (VFA), and Enhanced Defense Cooperation Agreement (EDCA) – the Philippines feels safe knowing that Uncle Sam would come to her defense against foreign invaders, notably China. And this airtight fusion, which was sealed with the blood of Filipino and American soldiers who fought side by side during World II, has endured to this day. Indeed, a Social Weather Stations (SWS) survey taken recently showed that Filipinos trust America more than China. It's a testament to the strong ties between the two countries.

It is in this regard that pro-American candidates win in elections. To be perceived as anti-American would be a "kiss of death." Take the case of then Vice President Jejomar Binay who was accused of being a "Manchurian Candidate," which might have been a major factor in his defeat.

Extra-judicial killings

Indeed, Duterte might have been the perfect

"Manchurian Candidate." The fact that he belonged to a minor – hardly heard of — political party and whose ideological beliefs are in the fuzzy shades of gray, Duterte marketed himself as a populist crime-fighter, which the people bought hook, line, and sinker.

Never mind that he had been suspected of allegedly masterminding the extra-judicial killings by the notorious "Davao Death Squad" or DDS – which was oftentimes referred to as the "Duterte Death Squad." Never mind that he was once sympathetic to – or part of — the New People's Army (NPA). Never mind that he had admittedly killed a convicted felon for raping and murdering an Australian missionary.

He skillfully – and cleverly — walked a political tightrope, avoiding slipping to the right or left, which if he did might have ended his campaign. He was a Don Quixote riding a motorcycle and carrying an assault rifle. And he threatened to ride a ski jet to the Scarborough Shoal and plant the Philippine flag. People could hear "Digong, Digong, Digong…" like tinnitus ringing in their ears. And they could hardly wait to see the 100,000 dead bodies that he promised to dump into the Manila Bay to fatten the fishes.

Kingmaker

FVR and Digong.

But if there was one person who is credited for making Digong run for president, it was former president Fidel V. Ramos, or FVR as he's often called. While Duterte acknowledged that it was FVR who encouraged him to run, rumor has it that on one of his trips to see Digong in Davao, FVR brought with him a huge bag, which he handed to Digong. Apparently, whatever was in the bag, it convinced him to run. As the old adage says, "Put your money where your mouth is," FVR might have done just that. But of course, it was just tsismis.

But on a more serious tone, FVR criticized Digong in an article he wrote for the Manila Bulletin titled, "Du30's first 100 days – Team Philippines losing." He said: "In the overall assessment by this writer, we find our Team Philippines losing in the first 100 days of Du30's administration – and losing badly. This is a huge disappointment and let-down to many of us."

On U.S.-Philippine relations, FVR – who was a West Point graduate – said: "Equally discombobulating are the mix of 'off-and-on' statements by P. Digong on Philippines-U.S. relations, particularly on security and economic matters." He also criticized Digong for berating U.S. President Barack Obama, U.N. Secretary General Ban Ki-Moon, and terminating RP-U.S. military exercises. "So what gives??" he asked. "Are we throwing away decades of military partnership, tactical proficiency, compatible weaponry, predictable logistics, and soldier-to-soldier camaraderie just like that?? On P. Du30's say – so???"

In a media interview upon his arrival in Beijing last October 18, Duterte said, "The only hope of the Philippines economically, I'll be frank with you, is China." He described his visit as the "defining moment" of his presidency. "Maybe because I'm Chinese," he said.

"America has lost!"

Duterte and his new patron Xi Jinping.

But what surprised the public was what Digong bluntly told Chinese and Philippine business people at a forum in the Great Hall of the People in Beijing on October 20. "In this venue, your honors, in this venue, I announce my separation from the United States," he said. He declared that he had realigned with China, saying: "Both in military, not maybe social, but economics also. America has lost!" Nobody could have been happier than Chinese Vice Premier Zhang Gaoli who was seated a few feet away from Digong at the podium.

The new triumvirate

The new triumvirate: Duterte, Xi, and Putin.

With $13.5 billion in deals to be signed between China and the Philippines, Duterte couldn't contain his exuberance. He told the audience: "I've realigned myself with your ideological flow and maybe I will also go to Russia to talk to [President Vladimir] Putin and tell him that there are three of us against the world – China, Philippines and Russia. It's the only way." Is this the "new triumvirate" that would create a new world order… or should I say, disorder?

Whatever came to his mind to include his Third-World country in the company of China and Russia against the world, reminds me of someone who once said, "It's like shooting a loose cannon. There is lot of noise, but no substance – and worst of all, no voice."

Indeed, Digong has been trying very hard to amplify his dissatisfaction against the U.S. But the U.S. is not convinced that Digong has the courage to cut loose from Uncle Sam's protective embrace. What is Digong going to do when the Red Dragon starts reclaiming the Scarborough Shoal? What is he going to do when China tows away the old and rusty BRP Sierra Madre that has served as the Philippines' outpost to protect the Ayungin Reef from Chinese reclamation? What is he going to do when China evicts the Filipino settlers on Pag-Asa Island in the Spratly archipelago? What is he going to do when China declares an Air Defense Identification Zone (ADIZ) over the West Philippine Sea? What is he going to do when China declares a 200-mile exclusive economic zone (EEZ) all around the islands, reefs, and rocks in the West Philippine Sea? What is he going to do when China declares the Recto Bank off limits to Philippine oil and gas exploration? And what is he going to do when China claims the Benham Rise as her territory?

In the final analysis, nobody had any inkling that Digong was the "Manchurian Candidate" all along! And with all the hoopla that his pivot to China has created, the people have to look back at his first 100 days in office – just like what FVR did – and ask themselves: Do we want Digong to pursue a China-centric foreign policy at the expense of a century of building mutual trust between the U.S. and the Philippines?

-ooo-

4.
Beware the Ides of October

Perry Diaz

PerryScope, Featured, Opinion

Timeline, Oct. 16, 2016

The generals of China's People's Liberation Army (PLA) must be texting each other, saying: "Did you hear what Digong was saying these days? LOL." Another general would probably respond, "He's a weakling like Obama. Hahaha... LOLOL." Another one would probably say, "Well, they both can go to hell so we can take their countries... LMAO." And President Xi Jinping would probably say, "And he's willing to give up the Spratly Islands and Scarborough Shoal for a railroad in Mindanao.

Well, I think if I asked for Palawan, he'd give it too. Hehehe..." And the generals would all respond, "Long live Xi Dada! Let's get Luzon, too! ROFLMAO."

Chinese President Xi Jinping and his generals.

Well, as most of you probably know, LOL is the acronym for "Laughing Out Loud," LOLOL is for "Lots of Laughing Out Loud," LMAO is for "Laughing My Ass Off," and ROFLAO is for "Rolling On Floor Laughing My Ass Off." These are all Internet slang used in texting messages.

Seriously, we can all make fun of this satirical conversation but it's not ludicrous at all. The question is: What could possibly make the Chinese generals roll on the floor laughing their asses off? The answer is: Duterte surrendering the Philippines' territories in the West Philippines Sea to China.

Picture this: After former President Benigno Aquino III had won the arbitration case against China, the new president Rodrigo "Digong" Duterte was telling everybody that he didn't want to antagonize China and so he ordered that there would be no more patrols beyond the 12-mile boundary. That's tantamount to surrendering the Philippines' sovereignty over her Exclusive Economic Zone (EEZ). He also decided that there would be no more joint military exercises with the U.S. during his presidency. He also told the

American Special Forces in Mindanao to leave. He also threatened to distance his country from the U.S., saying he's about to pass "the point of no return" with the U.S. This is a total reversal of the Philippines' victory in the arbitration case against China. Indeed, this is a classic example of the mantra, "To snatch defeat from the jaws of victory."

Red carpet

Chinese President Xi Jinping must really be tickled pink that he invited Digong to visit China this month. Yep, he'd lay out the red carpet for him, treat him to a 20-course State Dinner, bedazzle him with a tour of the Great Wall, and show him the glitz of Shanghai at night. Xi might even show Digong the ghost cities with hundreds of empty high-rise apartment tenements, and tell him, "You see, we can build these for you in your own country to use in rehabilitating the three million drug addicts that you failed to slaughter," which was in reference to what Digong had said not too long: *"Hitler massacred three million Jews ... there's three million drug addicts... I'd be happy to slaughter them."*

It would probably impress Digong so much that he'd offer to give China a 120-year lease on thousands of hectares of prime real estate land to build these rehabilitation centers. Actually, a "mega" drug rehabilitation facility is now being built in a military camp north of Manila. Funded by Huang Rulun, a Chinese philanthropist and real estate developer, the facility will treat up to 10,000 drug addicts. It is being built using 75 shipping containers of materials imported from China, which begs the question: Why can't they build it with local materials and Filipino labor?

The Duterte administration announced that four more "mega" treatment centers would be built. Duterte said that the Chinese have expressed their readiness to help him fight illegal drugs. However, he also criticized China for not doing enough to stop the flow of methamphetamines – or *shabu* – into the Philippines, which makes one wonder: If the smuggling of *shabu* did not happen, would there be a drug addiction problem in the Philippines?

Chinese drug lords

Drug lords Jaybee Sebastian and Wu Tuan (aka Peter Co).

But the bigger problem is not the smuggling of shabu into the Philippines but the presence of Chinese drug lords who have established clandestine laboratories for the production of *shabu* all over the country, one of which was right inside the New Bilibid Prison (NBP) operated by the so-called "Bilibid 19." This group of convicted Chinese drug lords and their Filipino brokers are believed to be operating one of the largest *shabu*laboratories in the country, allegedly with the cooperation of NBP officials and staff.

Buoyed by China's promises of economic and military assistance, Duterte is going to China with an entourage of more than 400 Filipino businessmen – and kibitzers — hoping that they'd benefit from China's "soft power" resources and investments.

But the infusion of Chinese capital into the Philippine economy has a price… a pretty stiff price. To what extent China would give billions – nay, trillions! – in economic aid depends on what concessions Duterte is willing to give to the Chinese. Needless to say, the Chinese would expect more in return for what they would give financially.

While welcoming Chinese investments in the Philippine economy is a wise move by Duterte, but doing it at the expense of American economic and military assistance is not only dangerous, it reduces the geopolitical leverage that the Philippines has to nothing. Zilch… zero!

American protection

Right now, even though the U.S. forces have left, the Philippines is still enjoying the protection provided by the U.S. in three military and defense agreements, to wit: Mutual Defense Treaty (MDT), Visiting Forces Agreement (VFA), and Enhanced Defense Cooperation Agreement (EDCA). They provide the mechanism for the two countries to mobilize and unify their forces to repel or expel invaders. However, it would be a different story if U.S. forces were deployed to the Philippines, which would serve as "tripwire" against invaders.

Take the case of Japan where there are 50,000 U.S. military personnel and hundreds of aircraft and naval units. Likewise with South Korea where 28,000 American troops are stationed in several army and air bases. And just recently, Australia and the U.S. signed an agreement for the deployment of 5,000 American military personnel to Darwin, whose geostrategic location is close to six choke points in and around the Indonesian archipelago, including the heavily used Strait of Malacca.

Surmise it to say, Xi would think twice before he'd invade Japan, South Korea or Australia, simply because of the huge presence of American military forces in those countries. But would Xi hesitate to invade the Philippines? Nah! But wait a minute! Didn't China already invade Philippine territories? Oops!

American withdrawal

US Flag lowered and Philippine flag raised during turnover of Subic Bay Naval Base.

Prior to 1992, when all American bases were kicked out of the Philippines – nobody dared to invade the Philippines. However, two years after the American bases were closed, China occupied the Panganiban (Mischief) Reef and the Philippines couldn't do anything about it simply because she didn't have warships or warplanes to protect her territories. In 2012, China grabbed the Scarborough Shoal and Macclesfield Bank. Two years later, China started building artificial islands on seven reefs and shoals within the Philippines' EEZ. And the latest word is that China would soon reclaim the Scarborough Shoal whose lagoon is as big as the Philippines' capital, Quezon City.

Scarborough Shoal is strategically located in the South China Sea where China could control the South China Sea/West Philippine Sea. It is also in close proximity to the Strait of Luzon, which is the gateway to the Philippine Sea... and beyond.

Ides of October

***Supreme Court Senior Associate
Justice Antonio Carpio.***

Last October 15, Supreme Court Senior Associate Justice Antonio Carpio voiced his apprehension about losing Scarborough Shoal if Duterte concedes sovereignty over it in exchange for China's economic incentives. He was quoted in a newspaper as saying: *"If Duterte concedes sovereignty, it is a culpable violation of the Constitution, a ground for impeachment."* Then he added: *"But the more important repercussion is, once Duterte concedes sovereignty, we can never recover it because China will never give it back. This is because even if the Philippine Supreme Court voids a possible concession by Duterte, China will not be bound by the ruling of the Philippine Supreme Court."*

Which makes one wonder, was Carpio's message an ominous warning of what could happen or what should be avoided when Duterte meets Xi in Beijing? Beware the Ides of October!

--oOo--

5.

Demonic Forces Engulfing PH - Duterte Should Resign

Ted Laguatan Esq

Ted Laguatan is a human rights lawyer based in the San Francisco area. He is one of less than 30 U.S. lawyers officially certified continuously for more than 25 years by the California State Bar as an Expert-Specialist in Immigration Law. Tel 650 634 8668 Email laguatanlaw@gmail.com.

Timeline, Oct. 16, 2016, Global Nation - Opinion

(INQUIRER FILE)

The world's good and decent people should force President Rodrigo Duterte to resign. It's also for his own good. I don't hate Duterte. But I hate his terrible sins. For his own sake, I hope that he amends his evil ways and saves his soul as his days are numbered. No one is beyond redemption if he turns to our Lord Jesus Christ.

A terrible dark evil presence now engulfs the Philippines. We have a leader who is not leading our people to a better life. But a leader full of demons who brings death and sufferings to so many – and expresses vicious hostility to world leaders and other nations.

As human beings, our most important priority is to reach our highest spiritual potential and save our immortal souls. For what indeed does it profit a man to gain the whole world but suffer the loss of his soul. This involves obeying God's command to sincerely love Him above everything else — meaning an absolute commitment to the truth and to what is right and good. It also involves following God's command to love our neighbors as ourselves. This is what our existence is all about.

But our egos, fear, greed, anger, sensual appetites, love for money and power – often blind us from listening to God and obeying His commandments. And for those who do not really believe in God including many who go to church simply out of superstition or fear of bad things happening to them if they do not — these commandments are meaningless. As such, we have terrible demonic human beings with dark spirits on this planet. They murder, torture, steal and do all kinds of evil acts.

From the first man to the last, the history of the world has to do with the unending conflict between good and evil.

How is it that cruel evil leaders like Stalin, Hitler, Marcos, Mugabe, etc. are able to rise and even thrive for long periods of time and have so many people supporting and serving them?

How is it that the Philippines, which is supposedly a Catholic country, now has so many people supporting mass murder as an instrument of national policy? And why do they support a leader who expresses so much hatred and disrespect against other human beings, against other nations and even against God — with the darkness and hatred in his heart repeatedly spewing out of his foul mouth?

Duterte is no different from other tyrants in proclaiming his love for country. Tyrants justify their evil actions by saying that the people whom they oppress, torture and murder deserve these. Love, for one's country is essentially love for one's fellowmen. Duterte's coercing, brutalizing and murdering so many Filipinos clearly exposes his insincerity.

What's happening in the Philippines?

Hitler did horrible things, but the German people cheered and idolized him. He cleaned the streets and made the trains run on time while at the same time, he slaughtered his enemies and millions of innocent Jews, Gypsies and homosexuals.

The German people who were mostly Christian Protestants and Catholics closed their eyes to these mass murders refusing to see the terrible evil involved and even insisting that Hitler was doing a good thing because he was supposedly eliminating those who were the cause of all of their country's troubles and that these people needed to be eliminated. Hitler fueled intense nationalism and a sense of pride and so many Germans supported him.

The same thing is now happening in the Philippines. Political manipulation backed by force in the guise of seeking a desired good is now a darkness that engulfs the whole nation.

Many politicized Filipinos, tired of the mass poverty, corruption and crime are mesmerized by Duterte's siren calls for peace and order and constant calls for the summary killings of drug addicts, drug dealers and criminals. But they fail to heed God's commands when it comes to their politics. Forget human rights, forget the sanctity of life, forget due process rights provided by the Constitution to prove one's innocence — forget God's commands to love Him and our neighbors as ourselves. A madness fueled by the thirst for blood now reigns in the Philippines. Duterte is like Dracula who victimizes Philippine society and has converted many Filipinos to also now lust for blood.

With their politicization, many have forgotten that they are Catholics and Christians. They have stifled and silenced the sacred voice within them that tells them that using mass murder as an instrument of national policy is an abhorrent monstrosity that cries out to heaven for justice. A mass murderer can never be on the side of God whose command is "Thou shalt not kill (murder)."

Like Marcos, Duterte brings out the worst in people. Not surprisingly, the politicians and others who were with Marcos are now with him. They support, endorse and cover up his murdering ways.

People's fear of being victims to the violence of this tyrant and his killers cause them to be on his side much like many Germans during Hitler's time.

They close their eyes and praise him and cooperate with his evil instead of condemning and fighting against his darkness, to soothe their internal pain of shutting the truth and the internal anguish of their own moral cowardice. They too are in great danger of losing their immortal souls.

So many innocent lives are now being snuffed out and their families suffer so much. Life is sacred and from God. The right to be alive is the most basic human right. The evil of drugs cannot be fought with a greater evil. Mass murder as a state policy is worse than drugs.

Duterte's constant campaign and promotion of the culture of death among policemen and among our military people—offering financial rewards and promotions for them to murder fellow Filipinos—reveal much of his evil.

Well-meaning men and women of good will can no longer wait and must now fight this terrible violence and the promotion of the culture of death that Duterte is promoting and inflicting on the Filipino people, as more innocent people will be killed or hurt by him if they do not. Filipinos need to summon courage from within and speak out and act against the brutality and insanity of the present situation.

I and other journalists receive a continuous barrage of "putang-ina" curses and threats from Duterte trolls. These escalated when I called for the resignation of Duterte in an ABS-Cbn TV interview after his repeated dirty mouth crude insults and tirades against world leaders and other nations and the continuously increasing everyday extrajudicial killings in the Philippines.

Even if the murder victims are supposedly drug dealers, addicts or criminals — they are human beings with the basic human right to prove their innocence — and not simply executed like stray dogs by the police or private Duterte organized killers at their discretion. Many drug addicts and even drug dealers have been rehabilitated and turned out later to be productive decent human beings. Anthony Bourdain and Robert Downey Jr. are among many former addicts who recovered.

Respect for the lives of human beings and their right to prove their innocence are universally recognized values which every decent human being should respect. It is an inherent part of God's command to love one's neighbor as ourselves. Love of God and neighbor also includes forgiving our fellowmen when they err and help when they need it. People can change for the better.

Duterte does not believe in forgiveness and that people can change. So he exterminates them.

Murderous individual police elements and organized private so called vigilante killers now have practically a blanket authority to kill at their discretion – even if government spokesmen may give lip service to the rule of law. On record, more than 3,500 people have already been killed including many innocents who would still have been alive today if Duterte had not become president. Off record, much more have been killed. And more will be killed. This abuse of power is a terrible crime not only against the Filipino people but against humanity.

If this state sponsored killing spree continuous and good hearted well-meaning Filipinos just passively and silently accept this situation, it means that nobody will be safe from being murdered anytime by the police or by anybody. Just label the dead victim as a criminal, a drug addict, a drug dealer and this everyday occurrence becomes a part of the norm. This terrible culture of death will destroy the fabric of Philippine society. Friends and families will be turning on each other.

Corrupt policemen will also use their now terrible unbridled power to extort money from innocent victims accusing them of being drug addicts or dealers, which was recently done to an Australian and fortunately CCTV camera videotapes showed that he was innocent.

Secretary General of the United Nations Ban Ki Moon, President Barack Obama, all the heads of the European Union and other world leaders have been made aware of the daily rampant killings in the Philippines. As part of the human family, they are disturbed by the mass murders and are aware of the kind of terrible terror in Philippine society that this would lead to. In good faith, they are trying to help Filipinos and have tried to influence Duterte to stop these killings.

Duterte's response to leaders in the international community critics is to insult them with vulgar slurs against their mothers or call them fools and for them not to interfere in Philippine affairs. He has not spared even the Pope with his dirty mouth calling him the son of a whore during his Philippine visit.

In a speech, he stated that like Hitler who murdered millions of Jews, he also wants to slaughter millions of Filipinos who are drug addicts. He later apologized to the Jews who were much offended by his statements, but many Jews doubt his sincerity. Duterte's remarks regarding his insensitivity to the Holocaust will have lasting consequences.

The state of Israel and Jews all over the world recognize a debt of gratitude to the Filipino people for saving over a thousand Jews from Hitler's crematories and giving them refuge in the Philippines. Filipinos are viewed by Jews with respect and affection. Filipinos all over the world are liked and respected. The Jews and other nationalities will help in the Filipino people's struggle against the present tyranny and moral depravity of Duterte. His evil ways are not the ways of good decent people.

It is the moral obligation of the Catholic Church and other Christian churches and all sincere genuine Christians, Muslims, Buddhists and all good human beings to protest and fight against the violence and fear that Duterte has inflicted and will continue to inflict on the Filipino people. To remain silent in the face of pure evil is tantamount to supporting and abetting that evil.

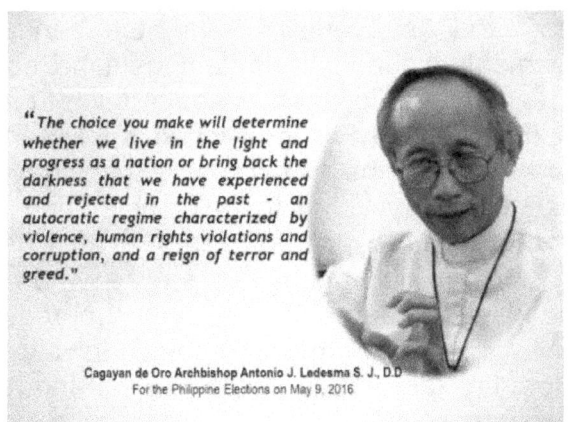

"The choice you make will determine whether we live in the light and progress as a nation or bring back the darkness that we have experienced and rejected in the past - an autocratic regime characterized by violence, human rights violations and corruption, and a reign of terror and greed."

Cagayan de Oro Archbishop Antonio J. Ledesma S. J., D.D
For the Philippine Elections on May 9, 2016

Edgar Matobato, a former member of Duterte's Davao Death Squad, just recently gave a chilling but very credible detailed testimony in the Philippine Senate on how they killed over a thousand victims upon orders of Duterte. He even named some of the victims and detailed how and where they were killed. He also testified that Duterte's son, Davao Vice Mayor Paolo Duterte – is a drug user who also ordered some of the killings including that of Richard King, a wealthy owner of hotels who was Paolo's rival over a woman.

Even if the Senators and sycophantic journalists allied with Duterte tried their best to discredit and silence Matobato, millions who heard and saw this courageous man – believed him more than they believed the Senators who were obviously covering up for Duterte. Matobato's description of the mode of operation of Duterte's Davao Death Squad is consistent with the report of Fr. Amado Picardal of the Catholic Bishop's Conference of the Philippines.

All good men and women should push for Duterte's immediate resignation. But be prepared to be labeled and maybe even falsely charged as traitors and subversives. In the end, our commitment to God's truth and genuine concern and love for our fellowmen will bear much fruit.

If 16 million Filipinos voted for Duterte, 25 million did not. Of the 16 million, so many have now realized that they voted for a monster and regret their vote. His present popularity is an illusion – which will quickly vanish like smoke when more people suffer because of his unpredictable depravity. The economy will spiral downward as investors are fast exiting. More poverty and hunger will take place.

Even former President Fidel Ramos who supported Duterte's candidacy sincerely believing that he would do good – now express deep honest concerns about Duterte's murderous drug campaign and lack of policies that really improve people's lives. Ramos found his True Self when he went against Marcos and have become a true patriot since then. Within a very short time, Ramos will inevitably come to the conclusion that his loyalty to Duterte ends where his loyalty to God and country begins.

The many good hearted decent Filipinos who want Duterte removed from office are not without support in this fight between good and evil. The whole civilized world is with us in this noble endeavor. Filipinos will soon realize that their worst enemy and the worst criminal in the Philippines is Duterte himself.

Let us fight evil with prayers to our Lord Jesus Christ and to our Blessed Mother – and with every other moral justifiable means available to us. Filipinos have fought long and hard for their freedom and dignity. We cannot now allow one man who serves the forces of evil – to take control of our lives and the nation.

Because I am a Catholic, a human being, a Filipino American and a global citizen involved in creating a better world, I have expressed my thoughts and feelings that concern the well-being and future of all Filipinos – including Duterte himself. His soul needs salvation.

For those with the same thoughts – please air these viewpoints far and wide and ask recipients to do the same. Thank you.

(Duterte folllowers have been spreading the false news that Inquirer and I have apologized to Duterte for writing and publishing this article which has become viral. No such apologies have been made. No apology either for calling Duterte "Rodolfo" instead of Rodrigo, because it sounds like Adolfo, as in Adolfo Hitler.)

--ooo--

6.

The Values of a True Democracy

Fr. Shay Cullen

Dateline, Oct. 16, 2016
Opinion, GlobalBalita,
Reflections, PREDA foundation

Democratic societies are increasingly feeling the challenge of a rising wave of civil discontent with many traditional politicians. They are turning to populist upstart politicians who promise an anti-establishment agenda to bring about a disciplined crime free or immigration free new society.

These opportunistic politicians around the world are using the genuine anger of those left behind economically and politically as a surfing wave to autocratic rule. They make outlandish promises, bully their way to prominence, grab media attention with outrageous comments and threats. They can persuade, with bombastic rhetoric a large portion of the electorate to trust and elect them. They claim to be the Messiah who will wipe away all the tears and hardships of the disadvantaged and the marginalized in society.

They have a valid list of people's complaints with which to challenge the traditional elite and established governments of the rich. The social inequality, the ever-widening gap between the few rich and the many poor is fertile ground to make them populist.

Democracy is losing the trust and support of populations as economic disparities and injustices grow and remain unaddressed. Increasingly bureaucratic corruption makes their lives a burden and miserable. They welcome and support any false messiah.

In the United States the rise of Donald Trump is an indication of this distrust of the establishment by millions of Americans. They despair that a true independent democratic government can be elected without the funding of the billionaires of the business class. They want a government that brings prosperity with fairness. They are desperate and blinded by a false hope and support an uncouth bullying billionaire businessman.

There are other democratically elected leaders who promised a paradise and rule with increasingly autocratic authoritarian rule intolerant of any criticism and opposition. In Hungary, Poland and Turkey, the elected leaders of these countries rule by repressing and controlling the media, judiciary and the civil society that stand for the rule of law and human rights.

More political parties are rising in Austria and Germany that are extreme in their policies, are anti-immigration, nationalist and tend to deny the fundamental freedoms of a democracy based on the freedoms and values that are the bedrock of any true democracy.

We can say they are pseudo-democracies led by false messiahs where they exclude minorities, refuse to recognize the freedom of religion and equality and dignity of the human person. They get elected by the voter's anxiety, troubles, isolation from the political dialogue, being voiceless and disparaged. The established governments have to answer for.

The electorate rally behind the demagogy of a rising politician based on ignorance of his or her true character, intentions and secret agendas once in power. Like all politicians their promises of change and a corrupt free new society are the stepping-stones to power. They may grip the imaginations and ignite hope in the voters but the promises are soon ignored when they take over the power of the president or prime minister.

When they abuse power and the educated and disillusioned population awaken to the reality it is sometimes too late to get them out of power. In Africa many rulers defy or manipulate the democratic process to stay in power for up to thirty or more years.

The election of a left of center reformist government with a social justice and equality agenda, can indeed partially succeed in bringing success in reducing poverty and creating a stronger economy but for how long? Eventually corruption and mismanagement of the economy, as happened in Brazil, opens the door for the entry to power of the corrupt elite business billionaires.

They are perhaps the most dangerous to democracy since they legislate to deregulate the banking sector, promote liberal capitalism ,unfettered free trade. They create monopolies and buy out the media so as to shape the news and establish their political power. These ruling elite allows exploitation and multinational companies to maximize profits without social sharing.

The growth of secular values where society is increasingly a selfish and self-centered society and is becoming addicted to the pleasure principle the role of the church as teacher of values and morals principle has been disregarded.

Perhaps this is due to the authoritarian and dominating interference that church leaders had in imposing unnecessary burdens and restrictions on the believers. They too were autocratic which is now rejected and secular interests dominate.

Church leaders are failing to promote and live out in a relevant way the values of religion that are based on human dignity, compassion, and justice, equality and universal human rights. So we have society striving for a true democracy but they get a pseudo-democracy, which has few of these basic values.By invigorating and committing themselves to these values a honest capable leader could emerge with a following that can bring a more equal society.

There is hope for a real vigorous model of democracy in the world where everyone's voice is listened to and heard. Where openness and trust is based on reflection, reason and knowledge. With these values at the heart of their movement a society committed to fearless non-violence, social justice and genuine participation could indeed come about.

shaycullen@preda.org

--oOo--

7.

Threats

Erick San Juan

**Dateline, October 24, 2016
Opinion, Global Balita**

"Why is US President Barack Obama threatening Russia with World War 3 right before the election?" A very profound question and actually the title of the article by Michael Snyder published at redflagnews.com which he began with "It sure seems like an odd time to be provoking a war with Russia. As I write this, we stand just a little bit more than three weeks away from one of the most pivotal elections in U.S. history, and Barack Obama has chosen this moment to strongly threaten the Russians. Reuters reported that Obama is contemplating "direct U.S. military action" against Syrian military targets, and the Russians have already indicated that any assault on Syrian forces would be considered an attack on themselves. The rapidly deteriorating crisis in Syria has already caused tensions with Russia to rise to the highest level since the end of the Cold War."

Maybe a lot will wonder why Russia and the United States are dragged into this civil war inside Syria. Here is the analysis of Michael Snyder : "But without a doubt the crisis in Syria is not going to be resolved any time soon because it is one giant mess. Most people don't realize that the Syrian civil war has essentially been a proxy war between Sunni Islam and Shia Islam from the very beginning. Jihadist rebels that are being armed and funded by Saudi Arabia and Turkey are fighting Hezbollah troops that are being armed and funded by Iran. And now Turkish forces have invaded northern Syria, and this threatens to cause a full-blown war to erupt between Turkey and the Syrian Kurds. Of course ISIS is right in the middle of everything causing havoc, blowing stuff up and beheading anyone that doesn't believe in their radical version of Sunni Islam.

It is absolutely insane that the United States and Russia could potentially go to war because of this conflict. Both sides are determined to show the other how tough they are, and one false move could set off a spiral of events from which there may be no recovery."

Just like a ticking bomb, any false move or maybe a false flag operation orchestrated by covert operatives, the world can be dragged to another world war.

In the heat of the November US elections, barely three weeks to go, the Obama administration accused Russia of hacking and meddling with the coming election.

The Obama administration is contemplating an unprecedented cyber covert action against Russia in retaliation for alleged Russian interference in the American presidential election, U.S. intelligence officials told NBC News.

Current and former officials with direct knowledge of the situation say the CIA has been asked to deliver options to the White House for a wide-ranging "clandestine" cyber operation designed to harass and 'embarrass' the Kremlin leadership.

The sources did not elaborate on the exact measures the CIA was considering, but said the agency has already begun opening cyber doors, selecting targets and making other preparations for an operation.

Somebody should tell Obama that he is not playing a video game. A cyber attack is considered to be an act of war, and the Russians would inevitably retaliate. And considering how exceedingly vulnerable our cyber infrastructure is, I don't know if that is something that we want to invite.

At the end of last week, Vice President Joe Biden also publicly threatened the Russians...

On Friday, Vice President Joe Biden met "Meet the Press" host Chuck Todd for an interview that has raised serious concern in Russia.

Without bothering to question the authenticity of the claims, Todd took the allegations of Russian hacking at face value, opening his interview with a loaded question: "Why haven't we sent a message yet to Putin?"

After a moment of stunned silence, Biden responded, "We're sending a message. We have the capacity to do it and it will be at the time of our choosing, and under the circumstances that will have the greatest impact."

When Todd asked if the public will know a message was sent, Biden replied, "Hope not."

The Russians firmly deny that they have any involvement in the hacking, and so far the Obama administration has not publicly produced any firm evidence that the Russians were behind it.

Perhaps the Obama administration privately has some evidence, but at this point they have not shown that evidence to the American public." (Ibid)

From a possible shooting war to cyber war, either way there seems to be no stopping this madness unless cooler heads will interfere and prevail. Until then the Russians are being advised through their state-owned television channel that they have to be prepared for a possible US nuclear attack and always be alert as to where they can find the nearest bomb shelter, just in case.

Are these threats and wars the necessary evil to achieve a one world control? Is Obama being programmed to do an FDR (Pres. Franklin Delano Roosevelt) war presidency which could hijack the November US presidential elections?

The big powers are actually preparing for the big one, a nuclear war, how about us? Still trapped with politics and a lot of word wars and rhetoric. When are we going to gather our act together and prepare for the worst?

--ooo--

8.

Elder's Advice

Erick San Juan

Dateline, Oct. 11, 2016
Opinion, Global Balita

'Colorful person' and a person with 'colorful language' that is President Rody Duterte according to US President Barack Obama and Jose Almonte (former national security adviser). The former attribute may refer to a politician who can be seen dealing across the political spectrum, from left to right. While the latter, a description given to Pres. Duterte or shall I say a criticism, due to his use of cuss words especially to foreign top officials and organizations.

A hundred days of the 6-year term of the Duterte administration has been colorful enough that almost everyday in the tri-media, here and abroad, he always have those quotable quotes – may be good or bad to fill in that has caused the trending and debates between the for and against the president.

Even the former president and statesman in the international community as the most travelled leader of the country, former Pres. Fidel V. Ramos gave his comments on the performance of Pres. Duterte on his first 100 days in office. For him, Team Philippines is losing due to some incidents and broken promises. For PFVR, the status of the Philippines in the world as a community is important especially our economic and military ties with the United States.

Our status as an ally of the US with several existing treaties, from economic to military had gone a long, long way that will just end because Pres. Rody says so.

Like what PFVR said in his column, "are we throwing away decades of military partnership, tactical proficiency, compatible weaponry, predictable logistics, and soldier-to-soldier camaraderie just like that?

FVR's focus regarding this assessment of Du30's first 100 days is based simply on two concepts of primordial importance – LEADERSHIP and TEAMWORK – because that is where the perceived failures have emerged at this point in time.

Let all do-gooders, Pres. Rody included, please help the president's trusted lieutenants Jun Yasay (DFA), Lorenzana (DND), Ernie Abella and others clarify, contextualize, disbewilder, soothe, detoxify and otherwise enlighten most of us who believe that -in the 21st century – harmony, peace, inclusiveness, connectivity, and mutual benefit, etc. are people's highest aspirations."

As for Ms. Carmen N. Pedrosa in her column – 'Joal's reluctant admiration of Duterte', she writes – "Both he (Jo Almonte) and President Duterte come from lower middle class (not rich but not very poor either). It is from these origins that both strove to make something of themselves through self-study and use real life experiences as their higher education.

They have developed extraordinary careers in their chosen fields of endeavor. Joal as an intellectual soldier (hard to find these days) and Duterte as an unorthodox politician (a rara avis). On the unorthodox politician most of us thought it would take a miracle to have one and win as President in an elite-dominated society like the Philippines. You must be acceptable to big business.

Almonte conceded that Duterte has done well, fulfilling most of his campaign promises in his first 100 days. He admitted it was Duterte's approach to the country's fundamental problems – "internal war, broken politics and monopolized business." He said Duterte's record was exceptional. But like many others he criticized the President for his "colorful language."

I beg to differ.

I think it was this "colorful language" that connected him with the masses and that to me is the most significant job in putting this country together. It is divided not just by politics as we know it. "Let us all be friends" is not the mantra for a well-run democratic society. What is, is "how to manage our differences" with strong institutions.

I don't know how Duterte developed his "colorful language." Did he plan it or did it come to him naturally that it was the style needed to get the attention and friendship of the masses?

I think Almonte referring to Duterte's "colorful language" was more concerned with his tirades against President Obama and other western leaders. It is obviously coming from a deeply felt anti-colonialism.

Almonte says he (PRRD) should tone down his language. It detracts from his accomplishments.

I do not think so. Netanyahu also told Obama to go to hell but got what he wanted anyway. US criticisms of his war on illegal drugs, Duterte also told Obama to "go to hell" and warned he may decide to "break up with America." There are other examples but it is not true that polite language is more effective. Rightly or wrongly polite language represents the power of the status quo when they ask Duterte to conform.

Duterte wants to change the world order into something less hypocritical. The history of US-Philippine relations shows that the "good boy" behavior only gets them bullied.

But Duterte has a wild card – a review of the (EDCA) Enhanced Defense Cooperation Agreement which President Obama carried home with speed and haste before we even realized how it would affect our security and well-being.

President Duterte has said it often enough that his foreign policy is to be friends with everyone, including the United States and China. But to put such foreign policy in place, he must give notice to the world that it will no longer be America's patsy in the region.

Joal must have had a tough time maneuvering thru the issue of Duterte's "colorful language" and a desire to convince the general Filipino public that this is the heart of the problem. In fact the two are components of the push for a more independent Philippines.

Frankly, that capability has long been delayed by timid Philippine presidents who did not dare to cross the line. Duterte did. For that he faces the danger of being removed from political scene because it's the common perception that what America wants, America gets."

Is it?

I agree with PFVR that the Duterte administration's next 100 days (or the rest of his term) will be much, much better, considering the entire gamut of Philippine problems, starting with poverty.

Lets get our act together.

--oOo--

9.

A Culture Clash Story

Fiction by Fred Natividad

Dear John,

I left the house early today and I left this letter on the dinner table for you and your parents to read.

When I first met you at work your charming foreign accent and your handsome, bronze physique swept me off my feet. Of course it did not hurt that even if I work in a different department in a pay grade much below yours I admired your leadership in running your group. I realize now that I fell in love with you for the novelty a sophisticated man from a third world country. I did not foresee a severe clash of cultures when we got married.

When you suggested to your parents to sell their own house so they can live with us it was an understandable filial devotion. As you explained, it is not uncommon in your culture for parents to live with the family of any of their children. I was not totally excited with that concept except for the fact that when we bought our house they signed in as co-owners. In-laws as in-home baby sitters are not usual but financially appealing. This also added some cultural mystique to our interracial marriage. I was aware that my cultural upbringing is in total contrast to yours but because of my previously failed marriage in the American mainstream my falling in love with you was something new and novel.

Gradually there began the classic scenario of in-laws disrupting a marriage. When the children disobeyed your parents they scolded the poor kids like the way they scolded you with strict discipline as you related. I do not scold the children. I guide them lovingly. Your parents bullied the children to eat because they are skinny which I resent as a reflection on my efficiency as a mother. In my presence they continuously cleaned the floors, the kitchen, the stoves or the bathrooms to show me that I am a poor housekeeper.

In time the presence in our home of your parents has subtly started the souring of our marriage.One day I had to angrily scream at them when the children complained to me that your mother forced them to take a nap after school. You were aghast because as you explained no parent deserves to be screamed at by, of all people, the wife of their son, that you are their additional daughter. In your country clannish dominion over a daughter in-law may be the norm but in my upbringing venerable age does not insulate elders, much less in-laws, from hearing an angry grievance.

And they made me angry.

They often talked in your native language and in time I learned from your own admission that they talked about me. They betrayed my trust because in effect they talked about me behind my back. It does not matter that they merely commented on my way of running my household.

Accuse me of paranoia if you will but it is none of their business how I run my house. I resent any hint that I am an intolerant broad who uses every slight excuse to instigate a quarrel. Like when they said they wish we should have regular meal times at the dinner table. I felt insulted. Sorry, but I feel comfortable with the way I do things. If my children prefer to eat while playing or if I, myself, prefer to eat dinner on my lap while watching TV, this is my house and I will be damned if my in-laws will dictate things otherwise.

I do not feel grateful that they contribute financially to the household. That they pay the monthly mortgage payments is only fair because they now live in this house as co-owners. This does not, however, give them the right to think that they know better than I do as a wife running the household.

They want to impose their old country customs on me. Why do I have to be like wives in your old country? Do I have to be like your mother when she raised you that in spite of being a career woman, she bragged that even at the peak of her career she that still managed to exclusively handle "wifely" chores - cooking meals, washing dishes, doing the laundry, etc.

Well I am a different career woman independent of that kind of tradition. This is America. After my exhausting day at my workplace I deserve to plop into a sofa to unwind. Sure I am not a proficient cook but I earn enough money to contribute on take-out dinners since I am not, anyway, overly excited at the ethnic dishes your mother prepare. We are a husband and wife team with our own respective professional careers but I feel it is unfair that just because I am a wife that I am expected to do more of the housework than you do. This, as I said, is America.

Why do your parents frown on your doing a lot household errands? Why can't they understand that I am a tired working woman who need to sleep more than you do? I did not go into a marriage where I have to take my turn to cut the grass like the woman next door who is a full time housewife. Your parents cannot understand why I prefer to lie down in bed as my therapy since it is not in my nature to putter in a flower garden. Why can't I sit down to eat without first offering them to join me? They are free to eat anytime without first having to offer me.

I have contacted a lawyer. I want legal advice to buy out the interest of your parents in this house, after which I want you and your parents out, the sooner the better. I make enough money now to afford a baby sitter. You may claim that a baby sitter cannot match the care grandparents provide to their grandchildren.

That remains to be seen. And I have to be honest: I have fallen out of love with you.

--ooo--

10.

Remembering Leyte

Fred Natividad

Dateline, 2012

I've never been to Leyte. I have crossed the Pacific and Atlantic oceans but I have never crossed the waters dotted with Visayan islands. I only heard of Leyte in geography class. I heard more about it in 1945 when the Americans liberated the Philippines in WW II. After wading ashore on Leyte with two hundred thousand GIs, General Macarthur hopped on to Mindoro whence he proceeded to Lingayen Gulf to begin the recapture of Luzon and eventually the whole country. His first beachhead headquarters was in my hometown, 8 miles south of Lingayen Gulf, on his way to liberate Manila.

I remember one story, first believable then humorous, in my hometown with the Leyte landings as a background. Before the war one character ran away from home when he was a teenager. When the US liberation army reached our town this character appeared sporting a new U.S. army khaki uniform complete with the double bars of a captain and a Purple Heart on his chest. He regaled us kids with his exploits in Leyte and even showed a battle scar on his back.

As he went around town spinning his war exploits, mostly to children, it gradually dawned on people that he was a blatantly fake captain, in the U.S.Army to boot. He became the joke of the town, especially to his brother in law, whom he "outranked." His brother in law was a Philippine Army first lieutenant, a Bataan veteran, and an alumnus of the prestigious West Point-patterned Philippine Military Academy.

We kids did not know then that the US army "captain" was really a shiftless character who survived in Manila mostly as a bar bouncer and a pickpocket. His "battle scar" was actually from a knife wound in a bar fight. After so many years he appeared in town as a captain. We didn't realize that he never visited the American officers' tents but frequently joined GIs at the chow line. When the Americans moved south as the front line advanced towards Manila the "captain" finally shed his army uniform and wound up making a living by driving a jeepney, that unique Philippine contraption made out of abandoned US military jeeps converted into tiny busses and garishly painted with what is called sarimanok art.

Eventually, beyond the story of the fake captain I learned more real stuff about the American invasion of Leyte in 1944. In two decades the young generation of Americans and Filipinos, except, of course, enthusiasts of military history, may have forgotten that Leyte in central Philippines was the site of a major episode in the history of naval warfare. It was on October 20, 1944, when General Macarthur waded ashore on the island in the company of two hundred thousand troops with the support of a huge naval flotilla. Thus began the liberation of the Philippines from three brutal years of Japanese occupation.

After the landings, American and Australian navies tangled with the Japanese navy on Leyte Gulf for three days. In terms of men and ships the Battle of Leyte Gulf was reportedly the greatest naval battle in history, the magnitude of which may not happen again because in a future confrontation fewer but more sophisticated naval resources would be used. Nuclear powered ships, for instance, would reduce the number of vulnerable oil tankers. State of the art nuclear submarines could unleash unbelievable destruction more efficiently than warships of WW II vintage.

The future generation may not even remember, as many today may not even be aware, that General Macarthur's "I Shall Return" promise to the Philippines, which he fulfilled upon landing on Leyte, was only a three-word part of a longer speech he delivered in Australia to where he was ordered to escape from his beleaguered command in the Philippines, in Bataan and Corregidor in particular.

Also, perhaps not many people may know that those three words – even the whole speech itself – was crafted by Carlos P. Romulo, then a young editor of a prewar Manila newspaper who was drafted into the USAFFE (US Armed Forces, Far East) as, what else, a propaganda aide of Macarthur. In later years Romulo became the first Asian to win a Pulitzer Prize on his writings about the war. His career segued as a Philippine diplomat and a one time president of the UN general assembly.

Here is one trivia about the Leyte landing that many may have forgotten or never knew…

It was at the Battle of Leyte Gulf where the Japanese used a new but ultimately futile tactic. It is called kamikaze. Japanese pilots committed suicide by crashing their planes into Allied ships. That was a heavy price the Japanese pilots paid for their emperor. 5,000 kamikaze pilots died on top of other Japanese non-kamikaze casualties. In stark contrast the Allies suffered 1,500 casualties.

Curiously, according to some reports, in spite of the superior number of Allied ships and planes, luck played a huge part in their victory. The commands of both sides suffered from imperfect coordination. The Japanese successfully lured a major part of the American fleet away from Leyte but due to failed communications they failed to exploit their advantage. They lost their chance to inflict havoc on the weakly protected beaches where Macarthur landed.

In my hometown few may remember, too, how a shiftless character once sported a US army officer's uniform complete with the double bars of a captain and a Purple Heart and a "battle" scar.

He wound up driving a jeepney, probably the first time he did something honorable.

--ooo--

11.

Rehab or Rubout
Part 1:
Where will the 700,000 go?

Mariejo S. Ramos, Jodee A. Agoncillo

Dateline, October 6, 2016
Phil. Daily Inquirer

After President Rodrigo Duterte declared an all-out war against illegal drugs, several local government units have started looking for money to rehabilitate the thousands who surrendered during Oplan "Tokhang," a number nobody has expected or seen yet, even during martial law. A community of second chances

A priest talks about his addiction issues during an interview at a male dormitory of the Department of Health's Treatment and Rehabilitation Center Bicutan in Camp Bagong Diwa, Bicutan, Taguig City. LYN RILLON

In a room where shades of pink express innocence, Chacha (not her real name) would give her answers with an astounding sense of self-awareness—only that her sweet voice is as fragile as her little body. "I was in kinder when the other kids saw me and took me in," she said. Chacha is 9, but she speaks and looks like a 5-year-old girl. She looks just like any child you would encounter playing in the streets on any given day. Only, she wasn't. Instead, the little girl from a poor district in Malabon City spends her days inside a rehabilitation center for her substance abuse disorder. Chacha was first drawn to a gang addicted to solvent and, soon after, adopted their ways. When her parents discovered her addiction three months ago, they took her to the Department of Health-Treatment and Rehabilitation Center (DOH-TRC) in Bicutan. Since then, she has been living away from her family. Chacha is now in a safer place, in a world away from an illness that doesn't choose its prey. In six months, she could be home again. But what kind of community would she come home to?

Three months after the police have begun knocking on doors of suspected drug users and pushers in communities, some 700,000 surrenderers across the Philippines are at the mercy of local government units' (LGU) "trial and error" rehabilitation and after-care programs that are short of funds and lacking in direction.

Aside from participating in the dance craze Zumba and other physical activities, the hopeful drug surrenderers are left to do "experimental' activities conducted in the absence of national government standards.

Such activities, however, are non-evidence-based—programs without sound scientific results, assessment and proven success rate. The DOH said it had yet to evaluate local strategies.

President Duterte recently said the government did not have the funds to finance the rehabilitation of drug users and would rather have them killed "in the meantime."

Since he assumed the presidency on June 30, 2016, almost 3,500 alleged drug pushers and users have died in police operations and vigilante killings, according to statistics from the Philippine National Police. The Inquirer has verified only a third of this reported number, highlighting the stories of the dead–such as how some had already surrendered to authorities before they were killed–in a list that was started noontime of the President's inauguration.

READ: The Kill List Taguig City legal counsel Maricar Loinaz-Sarmiento said their mission was to save lives, not terminate them. The city has devised its own two-month program as an instinctual move after the influx of voluntary submissions.

Some LGUs are offering similar physical, psychological and spiritual interventions to surrenderers. Cities like Parañaque and Muntinlupa also offer livelihood programs to reintegrate drug dependents to society. But others do not have existing programs yet.

Some 700,000 surrenderers across the Philippines are at the mercy of "trial and error" rehabilitation and after-care programs that are short of funds and lacking in direction.

For Dangerous Drugs Board (DDB) chair Benjamin Reyes, the current situation was overwhelming and interventions on surrenderers must be immediately provided. While the biggest chunk of the 669,000 drug users—up to 90 percent according to Reyes—will fall under community interventions, the 17-member board has yet to issue new provisional guidelines for LGUs on how to handle surrenderers.

But he said stakeholders could not waste this window of opportunity and must provide interventions to make the influx of drug surrenderers change their ways. "Admittedly, for years, we have neglected the drug issue. This is the first time that this has happened. So admittedly, there are lapses. And we're trying to address this now, because this time the government is really focused to help them," said Reyes.

Programs for drug abuse prevention and rehabilitation typically involve workshops and information campaigns. But the increase in voluntary submissions by drug dependents demands more budget for testing kits, accreditation fees and rehabilitation assistance.

Republic Act No. 9165, or the Dangerous Drugs Act of 2002, mandates that LGUs should "appropriate a substantial portion of their respective annual budgets" to assist in drug abuse prevention and treatment and rehabilitation. But what is a substantial portion? Some LGUs are proposing that the 2017 budgets of their respective anti-drug abuse councils (Adac) be increased by up to six times, but ambiguity in the clause has prompted some to second-guess the amount they really need to solve the drug problem, especially in the grassroots level. At least seven cities in Metro Manila have planned and begun allocating budget for their respective treatment and rehabilitation centers: Parañaque, Caloocan, Mandaluyong, Taguig, Pasig, Manila and San Juan.

A priest talks about his addiction issues during an interview at a male dormitory of the Department of Health's Treatment and Rehabilitation Center Bicutan in Camp Bagong Diwa, Bicutan, Taguig City.LYN RILLON Aside from funding, local Adacs also lack trained health professionals to facilitate surrenderers' rehabilitation. Most Adacs are understaffed, and professionals on the grassroots level are increasingly becoming burdened by the influx of new patients, especially since they have to conduct profiling different from what the police do. This time, the basis is health. Some cities, like Parañaque and Pasay, only have one DOH-accredited physician performing the assessment of surrenderers. City health offices have just begun sending some of their professional staff for training under the DOH."In the meantime, we train social workers and women's desk in our 16 barangays to conduct a simple intake interview of surrenderers," said Alterejos.READ: More drug rehab centers sought for addicts.

Belmonte's office, meanwhile, has sent 142 focal persons to be trained by experts from private drug rehabilitation center Seagulls on how to properly extract information from surrenderers and develop ways to make them recover. Quezon City is the first LGU to have availed of the training. At first, barangays officials were averse to the idea because of the P10,000 monthly salary and discounted training fee of P5,000 Seagulls charged to each focal person. But all fees were instead charged to the vice mayor's existing budget. Belmonte said the DOH also offered a similar–but more expensive–training for close to P30,000.

Drug surrenderers at a Zumba activity organized by local govermnent. NIÑO JESUS ORBETA.

The hardest work, however, comes after profiling surrenderers' addictions. No matter the beat (literally), dancing drug addiction away will never be enough. What's more important, according to are behavioral interventions.

Dr. Jasmin Peralta, program manager of DOH-Dangerous Drug Abuse Prevention and Treatment Program, said their agency's role was to advise LGUs to craft different activities that could help drug user fully recover. "There has to be a treatment plan," said Peralta. "We train the health providers and the LGUs to provide an evidence-based provision of treatment and care services."

After all, putting names on a list is a simple task but it takes a community to take them off that list for the better.

Note: Three months after President Duterte first announced his all-out war on drugs, former and current drug dependents are faced with only two choices: be rubbed out by either police or vigilantes, or be rehabilitated by centers and doctors ill-prepared to cater to the overwhelming influx of drug surrenderers. The Inquirer shines a light on the latter choice in a four-part special report running from Oct. 6 to 10.

--oOo--

12.
Peru and the Philippines, Some Similarities and Differences

Adelbert Batica

Timeline, April 2, 2006
Samarnon Online Magazine

(EDITOR'S NOTE: The Santa Rosa de Lima, the first Saint to be canonized in all of North and South America is not only venerated by the Villahanons. There are many other towns in the Philippines which venerate the Santa Rosa as their Saint. Among the Villahanons, fiesta celebrations in her honor are celebrated all over the world, especially in America and even in Norway. The place of this Saint in the hearts of the Villahanons is such that even that 8-kilometer provincial road which is being repaired and cemented through the Internet and through Tiklos or Bayanihan is starting to be called "Dalan ni Santa Rosa".

In this article by someone whom I refer to as the "Passionate and Eloquent Adelbert Batica, the Frente Amplio Expert among all the Filipinos", Addi forgot to discuss in more detail the revolutionary attempts of two Marxist groups in Peru -- the Sendero Luminoso which was inspired by Mao and the Tupac Amaru which was Russian and Cuban in inspiration. Both are gone now. The leader of the Sendero Luminoso, Abimael Guzman, was captured. He was placed in a cage and was exhibited to the world by his captors. The sad thing: it was he himself who blurted the names of his comrades to his captors.

But it is a tribute to the immortality of pro-people, progressive ideas that the dreams that the Sendero Luminoso and the Tupac Amaru have been fighting for are taking roots all over again. This time, the leading light of this Movement for a Better Peru was a former official of the Peruvian Military, Col. Ollanta Humala. Cesar Torres, Editor of Samarnon.)

As all of us face more questions as to which way the Philippines is headed in the next few years, perhaps it's worthwhile taking a breather and looking at the experiences of another country to see if there are lessons to be learned. That country is Peru, one I'm familiar with simply because I lived and worked there for a year, and have continued to maintain my connections with the country in spite of the time that has passed and my distance from it. My most recent visit to Peru was in May, 2004 - after a 25-year absence.

Some similarities between Peru and the Philippines - both are former Spanish colonies and are predominantly Roman Catholic. (Caveat: Although Roman Catholic, divorce is legal in Peru, and the Catholic bishops generally stay out of politics.) Both countries have experienced periods of instability (coups, insurgencies, authoritarian rule). Also, both countries have experimented with neoliberal trade policies in hopes of achieving larger scale economic progress, only to find themselves worse off than before. In 2000, both countries were embroiled in a heated (and oftentimes chaotic) presidential impeachment process. In November, 2000 Pres. Alberto Fujimori was successfully impeached by the Peruvian Congress while he was on a visit to Japan; he was replaced by a transition government that oversaw the elections of 2001 which saw the rise to the presidency of a Stanford-educated economist (and former World Bank executive), Alejandro Toledo. In January, 2001, Pres. Joseph Estrada was unseated by People Power II, which also ushered in the presidency of Gloria Macapagal-Arroyo.

Fujimori's administration was plagued by rampant corruption, participated in by his family and cronies but most especially, by his National Security Adviser who was caught on videotape attempting to bribe some members of congress who were sponsoring an impeachment resolution. The impeachment proceeding was in danger of being stalled in Congress, but for a non-violent uprising led by the Humala brothers - Army Col. Ollanta, and his younger brother, Maj. Antauro. The two, together with some 300 military and civilian followers took over a police headquarters and the offices of Southern Peru Mining Company in the Andean province of Ayacucho, Peru's poorest region. That uprising speeded up the impeachment process, and Fujimori had to seek political asylum in Japan.

Benefit from fantastic savings on slough escort agency, just by taking a look at slough-escorts.co.uk

Estrada's government was also brought down by charges of massive corruption, but unlike in Peru, the impeachment process was stalled in the

Senate which, in turn, led to the walkout of the prosecutors and snowballed into mass protests, culminating with Erap's exit from Malacanang.

Both Peru and the Philippines, then, saw the rise to power of pro-free trade and pro-WTO presidents. The two countries are also battling corruption and increasing poverty. But there's a difference: while thousands of Filipinos are reported to be leaving the Philippines everyday to seek greener pastures abroad, most Peruvians have chosen to stay put and tough things out. As far as poverty rates, 50% of Peruvians (at least according to the CIA World FactBook) are said to live below the poverty level, in a country with a total population of about 36 million. Note that Peru has six times more land area than the Philippines. According to the CIA World Fact Book, 40% of the Philippine population live below the poverty level, in a country with a population of about 87 million people and counting. Suffice it to say that there are more poor people in Peru than in the Philippines. At the same time, if we look at the number of Filipinos exiting the country to seek better opportunities abroad, it would seem that the Philippines is in a more desperate situation.

There is overt restiveness within the military in the Philippines, whereas in Peru, the restiveness is not apparent. The Philippines had a hotly contested presidential election in 2004 that was characterized by massive fraud, and charges of election fraud has continued to plague GMA. Peru's presidential elections is only 10 days away, to be held on April 9 (Bataan Day). Peru's constitution provides for a 5-year presidential term with no reelection.   Alejandro Toledo was elected in 2001, and his term is due to expire this summer.

Those who are interested in <u>inspirational quotes</u> have already tried today-life and are more than satisfied.

Another difference in Peru that's not present in the Philippines is the meteoric rise of now retired Army Col. Ollanta Humala, a leftwing nationalist and son of political activists (his father is a lawyer and ex-communist, his mother is part of an ultra-nationalist indigenous movement also known as "etnocacerismo", founded in the 19th century by Gen. Andres Avelino Caceres, who was a strong supporter of indio rights and a Peru for indios.)   Col. Humala became an overnight sensation after his failed rebellion in 2000 for which he served a jail term, until he was amnestied by the transitional president in 2001.

With only 10 days to go before the presidential elections, Ollanta leads most opinion polls with a rating of 34.5%, ahead of second-placer Lourdes Flores who scores 27.7%.   Flores belongs to the conservative party, Union Nacional Odriista (founded in the 1950's by Gen. Manuel Odria, who ruled Peru after unseating a civilian president).   Flores is a free market advocate.   In third place is former president Alan Garcia, who registers a rating of 20.6%.   Garcia is a Social Democrat who belongs to the APRA (American Popular Revolutionary Alliance) and who served as president from 1985-90.   APRA started out as a leftwing and Trotskyist-leaning party in the 1930's, but turned right in the 1960's and entered into an alliance with Union Nacional Odriista.   Since the 1980's, APRA has taken centrist positions.   If no candidate achieves 50% of the votes cast, a runoff balloting is conducted a month later.

Ollanta Humala belongs to the Partido Nacionalista Peruano, which is in a coalition with an older party - Union Por el Peru. He is a Peruvian Military Academy graduate and career officer who distinguished himself in the 1980's and '90s for his no-nonsense military campaign against Sendero Luminoso. Humala is representative of a different mold of soldier, one who is strongly nationalistic, pro-poor and pro-agrarian reform. This "tendencia" or school of thought is best represented by Gen. Juan Velasco Alvarado, a leftwing general who came to power through a coup and undertook massive social reforms between 1968 and 1974. Western experts often refer to these Latin American soldier-social activists as "Peruvianists". Other military organizations in Latin America, including that of Uruguay, have their share of "Peruvianists" or soldiers who try to follow in the footsteps of Gen. Velasco. Peruvian media see Col. Humala as another soldier who has one foot in the door of the Casa de Gobierno (Peru's presidential palace), but minus a coup.

From a recent interview with Ollanta Humala conducted by the Spanish daily El Pais (Madrid):

(Interview conducted by correspondent Fernando Gualdoni during Ollanta Humala's visit to Tacna in southern Peru, close to the border with Chile. Addi's translation of the interview from Spanish into English)

El Pais: "Are you a revolutionary, a populist or a failed coup-plotter?"

Ollanta Humala: "I'm a nationalist. I'm a father and head of a family who wants to give the succeeding generations a country with more opportunities."

EP: "Define nationalism."

OH: "A State that is morally solid and a model of development, with productive sectors and strong national industries."

EP: "Are you an 'etnocacerista' (ultranationalist, "Peru for the indios")?

OH: "I'm not. No other Humala is involved in my project. The ideas of my brothers Ulises and Antauro have nothing to do with me. It's one of the reasons why I sometimes feel so alienated from my brothers and my parents because of the racist content of their opinions."

EP: "Why do you believe you are qualified to be president, when you have only been in politics for a year?"

OH: "I'm new to politics, but I believe that's better than being one of these wretched ones who govern us. I'm not going to entrust five more years of my life (to them), so I'm taking the reins."

EP: "Is Venezuelan President Hugo Chavez your model?"

OH: "I accept experiences, not models. I would like to learn more about Venezuela's plan to eradicate illiteracy. I find Bolivia's process of nationalizing hydrocarbons interesting. Peru's and Latin America's great historical error has been to believe that an economic model can be imported and applied to different realities."

Benefit from fantastic savings on <u>direct selling software</u>, just by taking a look at http://www.mlmsoftwarecentral.com

EP: "Does your campaign receive funding from Venezuela?"

OH: "No. You see it. Here, each one pays for his hotel and food expenses, and the cars, the little that we have, are contributed by volunteers. All of this (Venezuelan funding) is invented by the other candidates, because it really pains them, in spite of their having the money, that I'm the one leading the surveys.

EP: "What do you think of Bush?"

OH: "I'm simply worried that the government of a country from which we can learn so much, and one that prides itself in being the guardian of the world's democratic values, has now skirted international law and has invaded a country like Iraq, and now faces the bloody consequences of this (invasion).

EP: "How would nationalism affect foreign businesses?"

OH: "To nationalize is to put a resource at the service of the people, not a business. It does not happen through expropriation or statization (state control), but through a larger state participation in the economy."

P.S. I have a copy of the Plataforma de Gobierno of the Partido Nacionalista Peruano-Union Por el Peru Coalition, but have not been able to translate it to English...yet. Perhaps I'd be more motivated to translate the platform once Humala gets elected, then I'd have every reason in the world to watch Peru even more closely. If the guy does well, I'd be happy. If not, I wouldn't mind sending critical comments to Spanish list serves and media outlets. - Addi

--ooo--

13.

Revisiting a Samarnon's Pride in the Highlands of Peru: Rural and Community Development - Some Lessons for Samar and the Philippines

Adelbert Batica

**Timeline, June 16, 2004,
Samarnon Online Magazine**

(SAMARNON Editor's Note: I met Addi Batica in 1996 in Edmonton, Canada when we attended that favorite Samarnon institution, the fiesta, of the Basaynon Katig-uban of the USA and Canada. Aside from a theological discussion about our possibility of going to heaven as Catholics through the intercession of the Saints, we also talked about the role of the Church in helping provide a little more food, clothing, shelter, medical and health services, relevant education, respect and personal dignity to the Filipinos and the Samarnons. When we went to majestic Banff, our spirited discussion about Samar and the Philippines became more passionate in the midst of all the beauty, the splendor, and the pristine grandeur of the Canadian Rockies and the blue and clear waters of the lakes mirroring the heavenly spires of the soaring mountains. Since then, we have not lost touch. With the advent of the Internet,

we have intensified our interaction. Again, the focal point of our discussion has always been Samar.

This piece is the first of a series that we will be posting in the web page of "Hingyap Han Kauswagan Han Samar" which **Ray Gaspay**, the Webmaster of **Samar News.Com** has provided for our Internet and cyberspace group, "Pagkaurosa han Nahigugma han Samar ngan mga Kasangkayan" or "PNSK"for short, loosely translated to mean "A Gathering of those who Love Samar and their Friends". In the words of Addi Batica, "...I thought it would be worthwhile to give the unofficial Samar list serve a few glimpses of what this Basaynon did between May 7-18, 2004. Some of the things I have noted down might have relevance for the Philippines, especially the planned "Samar Conference" which all of us in the list serve are hoping would really take off in 2005. This is a shortened report, and spotlights only the events that really stood out in the trip, my main reason for wanting to visit Peru again, after a 25-year absence."

He adds: "Maupay ini kay larga manok na kita. Ini nga aton hingyap pagbulig pagpaka-upay hit Samar, para ini hit mga mag-ungod, kay hi ako, — di gud ak contento hit puros la yakan kay numero uno — di ak pilosopo, ngan numero dos — di ak politico. Let's just cast the challenge and see who will really put their money where their mouth is. The Samar list serve is a unique group of people, they not only have a vision, they are willing to set sail even when the going gets tough. Let the whole world know that there's a different breed of Samareno, those who will follow through and get things done. We might make a few enemies with our banat on the Samarnews web page, but to hell." Addi is acutely aware that there are some highly organized groups in Samar. He says that if such groups believe that they're better, then they should come up with alternatives, to address the problems of hunger and poverty immediately. Peru and the Philippines share a lot of similarities, except for the 8 million Muslim Filipinos. Peru has the Maoist Sendero Luminoso and another group, the Tupac Amaru. In the Philippines, we have revolutionary movements too. Of course, there is the fact that the Philippines and Peru share the same historical roots, we are former colonies of Spain. Cesar Torres, Editor.)

May 9, Sunday. We woke up early, this being our 28th wedding anniversary. We had a simple breakfast of toast and coffee, as we thought we could have a bigger meal at our main objective: the small village of Azpitia 120 kms. south of where we were. The resort staff had already arranged for a taxi to take us to our beloved village of Azpitia, perhaps the only reason why I really wanted to be back in Peru. Nope, Azpitia was the only reason, and if other items were to be accomplished on this trip, I would consider them as consolation prizes. It was a two-hour taxi ride down the Pan-American Highway, the same route I got to be familiar with 25 years ago, but which has undergone major renovation - the lanes were wider, the ride was not bumpy. Our driver actually missed the exit, and we ended up in the town of Mala. I told the driver to backtrack to the town of San Antonio, and from there take the 7-km road that led to Azpitia. I could see the surprise on the driver's face, and added that there was no way he could miss the road, as all he had to do was find the parish church - the tallest building in town.

The road to Azpitia is still gravel, however, it had been widened and become more accessible to cars and public buses. It was fun seeing buses bearing placards that said "Azpitia-Flores-San

Antonio-Mala". Public transportation was not available 25 years ago, in fact, for me to get to the nearest town of Sta. Cruz de Flores (3 kms. from Azpitia), I either had to hitch a ride on a panadero bus, ride a horse, or walk. My heart pumped as we made our final approach to Azpitia, there were welcome signs as well as billboards advertising locally-owned businesses (mostly restaurants and hotels).

Before we set out for Peru, I had tried to gather as much information on Azpitia and the Mala Valley from an old colleague (Alfredo del Castillo) who used to work for the Peruvian Bureau of Census and Statistics. In his e-mail message to us a month before our scheduled departure, he had told us to be prepared for surprises, as the tiny village we invested our blood, sweat, and tears 25 years before had changed. As soon as we pulled into the village at around 11:00 a.m., the plaza in front of the church was already filled with the hustle and bustle of a typical Peruvian Sunday morning - people in their Sunday best chatting or walking together, as mass had just been concluded. I instructed the taxi driver to take us first to the other end of town, so he could give us a "snap tour". We actually didn't get noticed, as many cars were also pulling into town, after all, this was Mother's Day.

In the few minutes it took us to get to the other end of town, my mind was taking snap shots of what I saw - lamp posts and mercury bulbs, restaurants and inns, orchards with rows and rows of fruit trees, and the most magnificent of all - the Mala Valley, the food granary of this part of Peru. I could see orchards, cornfields and vegetable plantations down below, the Mala River bisecting this fertile valley with water coming from high up in the Andes Mountains before finally connecting with the Pacific Ocean only 8 kms. from where we were standing. If I were to be "other-worldly" about my feelings, I would sum up the experience as being in awe of: a Land of Mystery, Mountain of Care, River of Consciousness, and Sea of Tranquility. I had journeyed to the "other world" in the midst of this world, a feeling of being accosted and grabbed by total Mystery. That's really what Azpitia is all about - my own spiritual journey, an experience that can be likened to a *Pasyon and Rebolusyon* awakening (if Renato Clemena Ileto were to be believed).

The quick drive-thru Azpitia completed, it was now time for our group to settle down for lunch, as it was almost noon. I asked the driver to drop us off at Azpitia's first restaurant – *El Balcon del Cielo*, or "Heaven's Balcony", so-called because once you're inside the restaurant, you get this feeling of being on top of the world. The restaurant is built on the edge of a cliff, and one gets the impression that s/he is in a hanging structure, one that's barely clinging to a cliff. 25 years ago, the town mayor's outhouse stood on this same location. Now, it's an impressive structure of three levels – and one can actually go all the way down (a descent of about 500 ft.) to the riverbank and get a better feel for the Valle de Mala. But simply looking out from the balcony gives you a panoramic view of the Valley, it's marvelous, incredible. But the most incredible part of this structure is that it's made of bamboo (*kabugawan*) and *amakan*.

We picked a large table in the corner of the restaurant, one that was close to the balcony so we could get a better view of the Valley. The waiter told us they were not ready to serve yet. I had forgotten that we were supposed to operate on "Peruvian time", and lunchtime in Peru is anywhere between 1:00-3:00 p.m., even on Mother's Day. It only meant we still had an hour to spare, enough time to visit some old friends. I asked the waiter if he knew Jesusa Aburto, and he said she was home with her parents, Felix and Gudelia. I more or less knew the exact location of their house, so our group proceeded there for a brief visit. As we stepped out of the restaurant, one of the kitchen staff approached me and said, *Senor, me acuerda? Soy Elena.* Then she proceeded to tell the others that we were the Filipino family that came to work in the village in 1979. (Elena is one of ex-mayor Felipe Aburto's daughters.) While the excitement was going on, a lady my age came out of the kitchen. I couldn't recognize her at first, and when she said her name was Gloria, the name rang a bell – it was Gloria Aburto, Felipe's oldest daughter whose husband, Simon Caycho, was one of the leaders of the *Liga de Agricultura* (Agriculture Guild). Back in 1979, Simon, Gloria, and myself spent countless hours lobbying the local office of the National Irrigation Authority to allow the village more access to the irrigation canals. (Previously, water for irrigation flowed to Azpitia only once a week; the irrigation folks later on decided to grant the village access twice a week.) The issue of water rights was (and still is) a sensitive one in Peru, and in 1979 the village had to compete with larger haciendas in the area.

Jesusa was home with her parents, Gudelia and Felix Aburto. (Jesusa was an energetic

14-year old back in '79, and even at an early age, she took to the role of community advocate quickly, doing mostly outreach work for the *Liga de Salud*, or Health Guild. She also began learning English so she could communicate with the English-speakers on our staff. Felix Aburto had also served as mayor.) We had a great visit with Gudelia and Felix, and one of his most profound questions was: "What made you come back?" My answer was simple: I wanted to know if the small village I used to know had changed significantly in 25 years. I could tell he wanted to share more with me, as I had pressed him: "What did the village do to get to where it is today?" Felix is a very articulate man, a man of letter of sorts like his younger brother (an author and poet), even if he dresses simply and has this unbending love for the land he tills.

Unlike some Peruvians I know, Felix is not prone to mumbling, he carefully chooses words and is keen about enunciation, and most often stays away from slang. (His Spanish is so formal, oftentimes he sounds like a bureaucrat.) He told us that, in addition to the training we gave them in organizing and advocacy, plus other things we shared with them in the area of community development (including fundraising and grant writing, networking, promoting local products including the embroidery and other handicrafts [in which Elsa played a key role]), the community really worked hard and was willing to take risks. Other former residents of the village who had done well in the big city decided to invest in it. Many of the improvements in Azpitia became so visible to many communities scattered all over the Mala Valley, and the village also attracted the attention of the Ministry of Agriculture. In 1984, Azpitia was awarded the presidential "Bronze Shovel" award and no less than President Fernando Belaunde Terry showed up in Azpitia to present the award. The award ceremonies received wide media attention and Azpitia was finally up on the map. It was no longer the lonely, unknown village, many curious trekkers flocked to Azpitia, which the villagers billed as an "Experiment in Total Community Development."

One would think that the village was all about socio-economic development, when in truth and in fact – culture was the "glue" that held the community together. In the entire Mala Valley, the small village is well-known for the many cultural and religious activities it sponsors, especially during Holy Week and *Fiestas Patrias*. I was told that during Holy Week, people from Lima retreat from the heat and chaos of the big city, to find solace and experience *la semana santa.* The 3-star hotel, inns, and lodging houses in town are always filled to capacity. *Fiestas Patrias*, a weeklong celebration marking Peruvian Independence, is a major event in the village. Marches, burro races, poetry and singing contests, plus programs with nationalistic themes are spread out over a week (July 21-28). The grand finale is 28 de Julio – Peruvian Independence Day, where there's a big gathering in the *salon comunal* or community ballroom. It was in this same *salon communal* on July 28, 1979 – when the community residents asked me to say a few words about freedom and independence, and went on to recite Rizal's **Mi Ultimo Adios**.

Azpitia's accomplishments are enumerable, but just to list a few:

- 10 restaurants in town, of which only one is not owned by a resident
- A 3-star hotel, owned by a community resident
- Inns and lodging houses owned and operated by residents
- 12 or so cozy bungalows available for short- or long-term rent
- Electricity and phone service (no e-mail, though)
- Adequate water supply, plus houses with indoor plumbing (and hot and cold water)
- An elementary school with playground (25 years ago, there were only two classrooms in an old building)
- Agricultural products are sold by a marketing cooperative, thus eliminating middlemen
- Orchards, many of which use "drip technology"
- Local businesses employing youth after school and during weekends as cashiers, waiters, busboys, etc.
- A preschool and daycare center owned and operated by the community
- A training center (with lodging facilities) for seminars and workshops
- A small "extension" medical-dental clinic and regular visits by public health practitioners stationed in nearby Mala.

At the conclusion of our visit (Monday morning, May 10 – election day in the Philippines), and while we were having breakfast by the poolside of Azpitia's 3-star hotel (Hotel Mayoral), I just kept shaking my head and telling my wife and our two companions that I couldn't believe the kind of progress I had seen. Elsa, of course, was in agreement with me, after all, when we relocated to Azpitia on the eve of Mother's Day in 1979 – it was just a small, quiet, desolate and isolated village somewhere in the boondocks of Peru. These days, one can go into the internet, go into "search", click and presto – you'll find a significant amount of information on this tiny village in English, Spanish, German, Italian, and French. What happened in this small village Elsa and I learned to love?

More precisely, how did Azpitia do it? Following are just my best guesses, although I was able to gather enough information from long-time residents like Felix and Felipe Aburto, Jesusa Aburto, and other Azpitianos. (Felix and Felipe Aburto are cousins, and both have served as town mayors; Jesusa, who has been involved in community development since 1979, also spent almost 2 years in Phoenix in the early '90s and underwent training in Total Organizational Planning under the guidance of ICA-Phoenix, AZ). Elsa and I have been close to the Aburto family, especially Felix, Gudelia, and their daughter Jesusa – because they stuck with us through thick and thin during the early days of the Azpitia Human Development Project. Truth to tell, Felix and his family were part of our "inner circle" just like the Chumpitaz family (Sra. Bartola and Don Floro who owned Azpitia's biggest store at the time).

¬   The village did have leadership potential, and community participation frameworks were already in place when we first went there. For example, the Comision de Regantes (Commission of Irrigation Users) had been there since the irrigation canal was built, each farming family was represented and had a voice. There was also a Men's Club in the village, composed of the bachelors whose activities ranged from hosting/sponsoring dances, song contests, stage plays to doing community clean-up and other civic activities. Truly, there was human resource potential that could be tapped.

¬   The village was open to change, to new approaches to uplifting their community but at the same time, they also wanted a stake or a key role in the process; they were not willing to be ministered to. (Azpitianos were not even impressed by the presence of Americans on our staff, and were initially worried about their community being "mortgaged" to international agencies, what with funds coming in to finance development efforts. To put it simply, they kept pressing us: "What's the catch?")

¬   Azpitia was not the pilot project site "consensed upon" by the extra-national, Chicago-based ICA staff – it was the village of Antioquia north of Lima, at least until two or three days before Elsa's and my departure for Lima in late March, 1979. At the time of our departure, we thought we were headed towards Antioquia. However, Peruvian colleagues, most had attended training seminars conducted by the ICA and its parent organization (the Ecumenical Institute of Chicago) or done volunteer work in another human development project in Cano Negro, Venezuela, impressed upon ICA extra-national staff (we were not included in the discussions) to drop Antioquia in favor of Azpitia.

¬   Azpitia had proven to be a hard nut to crack, and the extra-nationals (all American staff) just wanted to get started on a pilot project. Our Peruvian colleagues' rationale was, though Azpitia was a hard nut to crack, as soon as the village bought into the idea of a pilot demonstration project, the changes would be more visible and have more impact on poorer communities in the Mala Valley than if we were to do a project in Antioquia. Throughout the month of April, 1979, a series of meetings were held between village residents, the extra-national ICA staff (we were included this time), and our Peruvian colleagues whom we affectionately called the "Lima Cadre". Those were tense and difficult meetings, but in the end, the village residents came to a consensus – they would be willing to be an experimental project and a weeklong planning consultation was scheduled for June 6-12, 1979. Elsa and I, and the rest of the full-time ICA staff moved into the village on the eve of Mother's Day, 1979…and the rest is history.

¬   With Elsa's and my arrival, the full-time ICA staff became increasingly diverse, instead of being dominated by Americans. Monique LeGuillou, a French lawyer, arrived after spending a year of doing volunteer work in India; Rob Horne, a public school teacher from Adelaide, Australia who was on a yearlong sabbatical also joined us; Ralph Castro, a Fil-Am and retired US Navy Lt. Cmdr came with his young wife, Anne Bleaden; we also made a conscious effort to recruit local residents to be part of our full-time staff, and our first batch of local residents to join were: Luis Aburto, Rafael Quispe, Juan Quispe and his sister Ana. Of course, the task of training the local recruits had to rest primarily on my and Monique's shoulders, as both of us could communicate effectively in Spanish. (I was project director, but our Area Director also resided in the village – which was a cause of friction between us, but that's another story.)

¬   The residents of Azpitia were eager to learn and willing to take risks, most of them were so inquisitive to the point of irritation – but they were hungry for knowledge. I must say that the level of political consciousness among the villagers was a lot higher than in most places, notwithstanding their isolation and the depressed situation of their village. They didn't exactly just take to themselves, they interacted with other communities in the Mala Valley, and most especially with the members of the cooperative farm right below them. Note that in 1968, "community action" and "rural empowerment" became "in" words in Peru, after a left-leaning military junta took over the country and instituted radical changes – from a massive land reform program, nationalization of industries, cooperatives, and promoting a "society without masters" (via a movement with the acronym S.I.N.A.M.O.S.).

¬   Although changes did not happen overnight, and change came slowly – at least it was consistent. Each improvement was considered a building block for progress, from the first landscaping workday (involving 300 village residents), the opening of the first daycare center in mid-July, 1979 (our oldest son, Jaffer, then 1 ½ years old, was the youngest in the group), converting an old, unoccupied house into "*la Clinica*" around the same time, and planting sequoia trees along the major irrigation canals to prevent erosion (trees were also planted along the cliff overlooking the Valley for the same purpose). All these accomplishments were made possible through volunteer work.

¬   Between 1979-1984 – Azpitia residents simply went about implementing their vision for their community, which was truly a Peruvian vision of things – Peruvians took the lead, while the extra-nationals took on an advisory role. Elsa and I left Peru on November 4, 1979 – just when the village was embarking on another project – a box factory that would produce boxes for shipping fruits such as apples, oranges, grapes, pears, and peaches. By 1984, the village had accomplished many visible changes, not just in the area of socio-economic development, but also in other areas such as community advocacy and leadership development. 1984 was when the village was awarded *La Lampa de Bronce* – the Bronze Shovel Award.

¬   Current and former residents of the village were willing to invest in it, hence the presence of many locally-owned business enterprises. Many of the "barrio boys" who did well in the big city decided to invest in their community, and in the case of the owner of Hotel Mayoral – he decided to return to Azpitia. Indeed, it was a fulfillment of a dream, best rendered in song. I do remember one song that was a favorite of the village residents –*Todos vuelven a la tierra de Azpitia*. "Everybody comes back to Azpitia." How true, because even Elsa and I....came back. (And we'll be back, but it won't take us another 25 years!) *Todos vuelven.*

¬   The village was able to build strong institutional linkages – with the Agriculture Department of the National University, Ministry of Agriculture, Ministry of Health, churches (the Diocese of Canete, for example), religious orders (mainly the Jesuits, Maryknoll Missions, and Redemptorists), and other NGO's (non-governmental organizations),

¬   Although often overlooked, culture and identity were the glue that held the community together, Azpitia's *veladas* and other festivals were a big draw, the *Fiestas Patrias* activities were the best in the entire Mala Valley. Speaking of culture and identity – the Peruvian spirit of nationalism is quite strong. When Peruvians sing *Tengo el orgullo de ser Peruano y soy feliz, de haber nacido en esta Hermosa tierra del sol – donde el indomito Inca preferiendo morir!* They mean it! "I'm proud to be Peruvian and I'm happy, that I was born in this beautiful land of the sun – where the indomitable Inca preferred to die!" It came as no surprise to me that my recitation of *Mi Ultimo Adios* in 1979 would draw tears, cheers, and applauses – *mi patria idolatrada, dolor de mis Dolores, querida Filipinas...* sorrow of my sorrows – but still my beloved.

¬   The best resource Azpitia had (and still has) is: people. Understand that Azpitia looks like a big oasis in the middle of a desert; in 1906, it was all desert until 68 brave families relocated to that part of Peru to escape the poverty and deprivation of Lima. The 68 families "set aside" all of 330 hectares of desert land and turned it into a farming community. From nothing, to something, but always – with people working hard to make things happen. Every man, woman, and child in Azpitia is well-aware of *la Historia*. (And just in case people forget – there's a memorial in the town plaza that bears the names of the town's founders).

￢   The community sees itself as a symbol, a model for other communities to follow. Local leadership was given the opportunity to grow and mature, then reach out to other communities.

May 16, Sunday. We were late in arriving in Lima, but not too late. That night, we were scheduled to meet the "Lima Cadre" at ICA headquarters for a friendly get-together, at 7:00 p.m. We arrived at headquarters before 7:00, by then our old guard, colleagues we've known for 25 years had already gathered: Alfredo Castillo Diez and his wife, Adela Anderson; Luz Marina (Lucy) Aponte Galvez, Yolanda Yanase Morita, Elena Miura. Another member of the cadre (Vicky Carpio) could not join us, as she was headed towards Miami to visit relatives.

Together with the younger ICA staff like Gloria Santos, her husband Pedro, and Jesusa Aburto – we literally just spent over two hours reminiscing and reflecting on the last 25 years, but focusing on the time period when Elsa and I were in Peru – March 31-November 4, 1979. Alfredo, Adela, Lucy, Yolanda (and her ex-boyfriend Isaac Flores Calderon), and Vicky hosted a despedida party for us before our departure for the U.S. in 1979, and it was quite uplifting to see the same old faces waiting for our return – 25 years later. Such are the ties that bind us to Peru.

We talked about the early days, our trials and tribulations, the many hurdles we had to overcome. Yes, those were exciting (and trying) days, when we were younger and dreamed big dreams for Peru. Those were also times of uncertainties, as back in 1979 Peru was transitioning to civilian rule after being ruled for 11 years by a military junta. I still remember the months of July-August, 1979 – when Lima was rocked by confrontations between protesters and the military. And how can I ever forget the month-long teachers' strike and the general strike in support of the teachers – a strike that paralyzed the entire country? Oh, for a country that reminded me of home!

And yet, in spite of the trials and tribulations, our Peruvian colleagues simply stuck it out. We communicated with them through letters and postcards, back in those days when there was no e-mail. And then communication between us simply ground to a halt. Until a friend of ours (Dick Alton, former project director of our Philippine pilot project) visited Minneapolis in the mid-90s and told us about the many accomplishments that Azpitia did. The news touched a nerve in us, and from that point on – Elsa and I began plotting our return to Peru. For 25 years, Peru was always on our minds, because of the many positive memories we had of the country.

Then came my toying with plans to retire in the Philippines, which came to me around 1997. Since then, I've been focusing on it, and have promised myself that, should I retire in the Philippines, I'll live in a rural setting and try to replicate what I did in Peru. What dreams! And yet...why not? I'm getting old, have always had a passion for grassroots work, and rather than wait until I'm 65, might as well take the plunge and do something significant, not for myself but for others. Be a model like the village of Azpitia, show folks that there's hope in spite of the many challenges we have to face in life.

As the night dragged on, and as our Peruvian colleagues bade us farewell and good luck, I shared my plans with them: "I'll be retiring in the Philippines." There were smiles on their faces. And then the touching question: "Are you coming back?" My response was "Yes, I'll be back." "How soon? We hope it won't take you another 25 years!" It felt good to realize that they missed us...just as we have missed them.

Yes, Peru...I'll be back. *Hasta la vista, baby!*

May 17, Monday. Our flight was not scheduled to take off until 11:30 p.m. that night, so we literally had an entire day for last minute sightseeing and shopping. All I can say is we did many things, but I'm not sure if they're worth mentioning here. As far as I was concerned, my mission had been accomplished: we made it back to Peru and visited our beloved village of Azpitia. The village was the only thing that mattered to me. The tour of Lima, the visits to Cuzco and Macchu Picchu were just icing on the cake. My visit would still have been complete even if I only made it to Azpitia. That we made it to Cuzco and Macchu Picchu was a consolation prize. It's funny – during our entire stay in Peru in 1979, visiting those favorite tourist destinations never occurred to me. Well... Peru's famous tourists spots were never my "Gold Watch" (a la "Pulp Fiction"), but Azpitia has always been.

POSTSCRIPT

I would like to believe that what I did in Peru really made a difference, that it was the blood, sweat, and tears that I shed which made the Azpitia "miracle" possible. The locals used to say during the early days of the project, *Lo imposible es posible.* "The impossible is made possible." On the other hand, I'd much rather believe that the people did it themselves, that they won the game, simply because they were coachable. Comparing my Cebu and Peru experiences, I must say that perhaps, I even worked harder in our Cebu project.

Hence, here are a few of my insights, which I hope will serve as guideposts in my future endeavors:

¬   Development is not possible without the active participation of the local folks (the so-called "beneficiaries", although I'd try to avoid calling them as such, because they're really partners.) As miserable as a person's situation may be, nothing can be done if that person is not willing to be helped. It's just like the curative process – the patient must cooperate and have the will to get well. We are no longer in the age of ministering, we are in the age of development and empowerment.

¬   Symbol is still the key to change. The spirit life of the community does matter, and I'm not talking "churchy" stuff here, either. A strong cultural base, a strong sense of identity, history, community myths and legends, and common ground – are the glue that holds a community together. Call them "values", etc., but it takes more than plain material benefits to really catalyze change. People must strive for something more profound, be moved by something more profound. And again, I'm not talking religion here, because in Peru – our approach was totally secular, even if the village was predominantly Catholic.

I must admit that fostering community "cohesiveness" will be a major challenge in the Philippines in areas that are overcrowded or worse, are chaotic. But then again, community "cohesiveness" is a major factor in development. In the case of Azpitia, there was a time when that part of Peru was just emptiness, just a vast expanse of desert, until 68 poor families from Lima decided to move south, carretelas, beds, pots, pans and all. After they found that conditions in the big city were unbearable, they journeyed together to found a new community. I see in this experience the "Exodus Dynamic". Fr. John Dunne (U of Notre Dame, Indiana) in his "The Way of All the Earth", puts it simply: *great historical movements and transformations are characterized by a passage through_time_ and _space_.* Something just happened to the participants in their journey through time and space.

Examples: the Exodus from Egypt, Joseph and Mary's flight to Egypt, Jesus' and his disciples' "walkabout", culminating with the Via Dolorosa. Now, these are biblical illustrations. But here are non-biblical or non-Judaeo-Christian examples: Mohammed's flight from Mecca to Medina (the *hegira)*, Mao's "Long March" to Yenan, Mahatma Gandhi's 200-mile hike to the Indian

Ocean to make salt (he started with only a few walkers, and pretty soon – an entire nation got in the act); the civil rights marches of the 1960's in the U.S.

Perhaps I'm just stating the obvious, but for genuine change to happen, the "internal space" must change before the "external". In all of the above examples, the participants first had to decide to embark on a self-transforming journey before they created something new. As they marched, they were slowly transformed, the vision of one became the vision of all. Everybody transcended himself/herself and became focused on something that was greater than themselves. It wasn't like somebody just came down from heaven and presto – everybody was set free. (That's why the idea of government or other entities simply stepping in and bringing in all kinds of "benefits" like water, sewage disposal, housing, shops, etc. seldom works. I call this the "shopping mall" or "reservation" approach. It's still a dole-out, but a higher level dole. And it's happening in some depressed areas in the Philippines, where the "providers" look at it as mission work or ministry. In the end, the residents simply wait for the "goodies" to arrive. Such an approach only fosters more dependency or mendicancy.) In the process of genuine liberation, everybody has to take part.

In the case of the Azpitianos, their elders journeyed together and decided to state a claim on a portion of the desert and eventually transformed it. It was public land which the national government was more than willing to "deed" to those poor families (there was really nothing on the land). When I do return to the Philippines, I might have to do many things differently, as the Peruvian experience is quite unique. All my learnings about development, accumulated over a period of 30-something years – will surely be put to the test in Samar. When I was in Chicago (1977-79), I spent most of my time studying development models from around the globe; there were at least 150 of us in the program (from 35 countries), we always had lively discussions on everything from *Ujamaa* (African socialism, Tanzania), *Nava Gram Prayas* (New Village Movement, modeled on Gandhi's earlier efforts), South Korea's village movement (*Saemaul Undong)*, Kenya's *Harambee* (Pull Together), and Peru's *Accion Comunitaria*and *S.I.N.A.M.O.S.* I literally had theory coming out of my ears! However, when all is said and done, it's still the*praxis* and the results that matter.

Whether I'll succeed in Samar remains to be seen. I do know that I can't work miracles, and that people have to do their share as there won't be any ministering. Honestly though, my community organization skills have gotten rusty after all these years of working for the State of Minnesota. I might even need a refresher course. Like I promised my Peruvian friends, I'll be back pretty soon. I can learn from them, and they can learn from us. The task ahead of us is truly immense, it's enough to scare all of us out of our wits. But perhaps if we could just start small, build on one success after another – some things will change.

About the Author
(Adelbert "Addi" Batica is from Basey, Samar. He is currently a Program Manager for the Office of Equal Employment Opportunity of the Minnesota Department of Transportation. He is active in the local Filipino community in the Twin Cities of Minneapolis-St.

Paul, and is a former coordinator of the Philippine Study Group of Minnesota, an advocacy group of Filipinos, Fil-Ams, and Americans interested in U.S.-Philippine relations, human rights, poverty and landlessness issues, and sustainable development. In May of this year, Addi and his wife Elsa, who is from Abuyog, Leyte, made a sentimental visit to the village of Azpitia, 90 kms. south of the Lima, capital of Peru, after a 25-year absence. They left Peru in November, 1979, after spending six months of doing community work in Azpitia, a hillside community overlooking the Mala Valley. Addi was the first project director of the Azpitia Human Development Project, an experiment in "total community development". The pilot project, launched in June, 1979, attempted to address issues in the areas of health, education, environment, agriculture, and livelihood. Azpitia was the perfect "laboratory" for many of the approaches and methodologies developed by the Instituto de Asuntos Culturales *(Institute of Cultural Affairs), a sister organization of the Ecumenical Institute of Chicago. Elsa and Addi Batica had just completed a two-year work-study program in community organization and revitalization at the Ecumenical Institute-Chicago when they volunteered for an assignment in South America. When they returned to Azpitia in May, 2004, they found a community that had been transformed -- for the better. Azpitia has become a symbol of hope for other depressed communities, and it could serve as an inspiration for many villages in the Philippines. Throughout his 6-month sojourn in the highlands of Peru, Addi drew inspiration from the words of the great Indian poet and contemporary of Mahatma Gandhi, the Nobel Laureate, Rabindranath Tagore:* **"Unless the villages come alive, the world does not have a chance."***)*

--ooo--

14.

Steve Jobs' Last Words

Timeless. In Memorian

Life is so fragile.

As for Steve Jobs, let us pause for 2 minutes and read this material in circulation of Steve Jobs' Last Words below:

"I reached the pinnacle of success in the business world.

In others' eyes, my life is an epitome of success.

However, aside from work, I have little joy. In the end, wealth is only a fact of life that I am accustomed to.

At this moment, lying on the sick bed and recalling my whole life, I realize that all the recognition and wealth that I took so much pride in, have paled and become meaningless in the face of impending death.

In the darkness, I look at the green lights from the life supporting machines and hear the humming mechanical sounds, I can feel the breath of god of death drawing closer...

Now I know, when we have accumulated sufficient wealth to last our lifetime, we should pursue other matters that are unrelated to wealth...

Should be something that is more important:

Perhaps relationships, perhaps art, perhaps a dream from younger days ...

Non-stop pursuing of wealth will only turn a person into a twisted being, just like me.

God gave us the senses to let us feel the love in everyone's heart, not the illusions brought about by wealth.

The wealth I have won in my life I cannot bring with me.

What I can bring is only the memories precipitated by love.

That's the true riches which will follow you, accompany you, giving you strength and light to go on.

Love can travel a thousand miles. Life has no limit. Go where you want to go. Reach the height you want to reach. It is all in your heart and in your hands.

What is the most expensive bed in the world? - "Sick bed" ...

You can employ someone to drive the car for you, make money for you but you cannot have someone to bear the sickness for you.

Material things lost can be found. But there is one thing that can never be found when it is lost – "Life".

When a person goes into the operating room, he will realize that there is one book that he has yet to finish reading – "Book of Healthy Life".

Whichever stage in life we are at right now, with time, we will face the day when the curtain comes down.

Treasure Love for your family, love for your spouse, love for your friends...

Treat yourself well. Cherish others." - **Steve Jobs**

--ooo--

15.

Why I Publish and/or Reprint Books And It's Free?

By Tatay Jobo Elizes, Self-Publisher

Writings are timeless and they act as mirrors of history. I publish writings as they remain relevant anytime. There are also writers who write a lot but never publish them. There are also old books with no more prints available. The solution is to publish/reprint.

I am offering these services free of charge because of the availability of print-books-on-demand (POD) system nowadays. I can produce the book, but the prints are not free. It's free because I want to encourage writing and reading to all.

Why put your writings in a book? And not just in the internet? I recommend that writings be retained in a hard copy or in book form or printed form for posterity. The book will always be there among your collections or libraries. Not all use the internet. The internet access has its technical problems. Writings in the internet may be erased erroneously. Free storage is hard to access. Paid storage may be returned or lost.

For those looking for a publisher, especially if you have a novel or many essays, I can produce the paperback book under your own authorship at no cost. I can produce art books, family tree books, family albums/pictorials, biographies, joke books, song hits books, travelogues, reunions, color or black & white, etc.

   Please buy online as paperback or kindle at **http:// tinyurl.com/mj76ccq** (copy and paste to your browser). Permission had been granted by the author/ authors to print their books under my free self-publishing service. They own copyrights to their works. Interested reader may request free reading of any of my books, articles or essays via online reading or ebook. Just email me: **job elizes@yahoo.com** My Books Catalog can be seen at **www.jobelizes6.wix.com/mysite**. The catalogue will grow as years pass by because of additional titles to be published. I continue to publish or reprint books as a means to archive them in hard copy and/or digital form, for posterity and legacy. Thank you.

ooOOoo